The Best
and
The Brightest

The Best and The Brightest

David N. Aspy

 Human Resource Development Press

LB
2832.2
.A85
1984

*Human
Resource
Development
Press*

R00479 53068

Copyright © 1984 by Human Resource Development Press, 22 Amherst Road, Amherst, Massachusetts 01002. (413) 253-3488. All rights reserved. No part of the material protected by this copyright notice may be reproduced or utilized in any form or by any means, electronic or mechanical, including photocopy, recording, or by any information storage and retrieval system, without permission from the copyright owner.

ISBN Number   0-914234-76-5

Library of Congress Cataloging in Publication Data

First Edition
First Printing, May 1984

Manufactured in the United States of America

Preface

Would you like to be a teacher? I mean a professional teacher who teaches a room full of students for at least six hours a day, five days a week. Sound exciting? Some people find it exhilarating and challenging. Believe it or not.

Why would people find teaching exciting? Don't they know that newspapers, television, radio, and government officials are denigrating the schools? Don't they know that parents and students are crying that teachers are lousy? Is it that teachers don't understand what's going on, or maybe the people who like to teach are just martyrs who like to suffer? They might as well suffer for school children.

The truth is that despite the swirl of criticism about schools and teachers, we can find some very effective teachers who are helping students learn. Often they are doing it in spite of the denigration that is being heaped upon them. They are not dumb. They are bright. They are not bleeding hearts. They are sound minded. They are not rejects from society. They are effective people. They are not untrained. They have a large repertoire of skills. In short they are some of America's best and brightest.

Why all of the hubbub about the quality of our schools? The reasons are varied. For example, some politicians have decided to use education as an issue in their campaigns. These opportunistic characters will continue to come and go in the educational struggle, and will leave behind them confusion rather than problem resolution.

Preface

Some business people are interested in schools because they need qualified workers for their establishments. These people cry for more vocational training, and advise students that not everyone needs a college-oriented education.

Some in the military establishment assert that education should prepare people to defend the nation. They contend that the country is in real trouble if it is defended by people who can't read.

Some religious groups maintain that schools should teach values, while similar groups believe they should leave this type of teaching to parents. Both of these groups state that America's decline is rooted in its failure to teach values.

Some scientists have said that unless we teach more science to our students we are doomed to failure as a society. These people point to the success of the Japanese people and advocate an effort to match and surpass them. These comments and others are repeated often. Nearly everyone knows what schools should or should not be doing. In America we safeguard the right of everyone to state his or her opinion about education or any other topic and thus educators are bombarded with comments and suggestions. The resulting cacophony surrounding education is nearly deafening. Yet, in the midst of the chaos we find some stalwart people holding schools together. To the degree that schools are the cornerstone of society, these fine educators are also holding together the building blocks (foundations?) of our future.

Who are these educators who are holding us together? They are teachers, principals, professors and college administrators. They can be found at all levels of American Education. The trouble is that most of us don't know how to identify them. In too many instances, critics don't have the skills to discriminate between effective and ineffective teachers. Therefore, too often an assault upon education sweeps out the wheat with the chaff, the good with the bad. Because of their ineptitude, many would-be reformers do more harm than good, and education is left amid the rubble of a good-intentioned roadway.

This chaotic situation will cease only when the various publics served by schools acquire the skills of discriminating between effective and ineffective teaching. Until these skills are acquired and used, education will continue to be the periodic victim of a tug-of-war between various unskilled pressure groups. The wonder of it all is how well the schools have progressed.

Effective teaching is a result of the implementation of specific skills. These skills are identifiable and subject to training intervention. They can

Preface

be summarized as: (a) developing the subject matter content, (b) lesson planning, (c) developing methods of teaching delivery, (d) delivering content and (e) relating effectively to students interpersonally.

With sufficient descriptions of these skills, we can enter a learning context and make discriminations between ineffective and effective teachers. Such findings will be more than emotionalized response; they will be informed, objective data which can be translated into growth programs for individual teachers. This is a constructive approach to improving education which can replace the present process that is destructive in too many instances.

Fortunately, some exemplars of teaching have been identified in previous studies. These people actually exist. They can be found in classrooms across America. The exemplar teachers have risen above the chaos surrounding education and continued in their constructive paths. Their stories give us "real-life" models of what is possible for many learners, teachers and schools. Truly, these people are among the best and brightest of teachers. They are also among the best and brightest of citizens. The remainder of this book presents profiles of some of these exemplars.

It is hoped that their stories and skills evaluations will help in identifying more exemplars. Acquisition of these skills can be used to help teachers develop into exemplars. The present cacophony of educational criticism can be replaced with a symphony of growth. That is what education is all about. Through skills, we can become at least informed critics of education and at best constructive contributors to it.

Amherst, Massachusetts **D.N.A.**

To The Reader

Each story in *The Best and The Brightest* is about a real person and a real life. In every case, the events depend upon human decision and achievement, not the intervention of an author. After all, true stories allow us to enter into real lives and be observers. If we read well, we may integrate what we learn into our own lives.

What has also been attempted in *The Best and The Brightest* is a presentation of whole people, not merely lists of chronological events. Where appropriate, I have encouraged the teacher's voice to come through and be heard above the sound of the text: Clifton's creative energy, Hila's faith or Mack's powerful vision and strength. In a real sense I have only translated these stories into a cohesive text. If I've succeeded, you are about to meet these eight people as I know them, and to hear the sound of their voices.

Amherst, Massachusetts   **D.N.A.**

Contents

1. Actualizing The Dream / *Clifton Sparks*   1
2. Sustaining The Promise / *John McFarland*   11
3. Crossing Boundaries / *Marisa Valderas*   21
4. Implementing A Mission / *Hila Pepmiller*   31
5. Growing With The Team / *Carl Tatum*   41
6. Using Personal Power / *Flora Roebuck*   49
7. Combining Strength and Facilitation / *Andy Griffin*   59
8. Giving It All / *Mack Harris*   69
9. Putting It Into Perspective / *Summary*   77
10. Exemplar Teaching / *Some Afterthoughts*   85

1 / Actualizing the Dream

Clifton Sparks

As Martin Luther King, Jr. rose to the podium, Clifton's eyes filled with tears. Her body tingled with joy and expectation. She knew that an unforgettable moment was approaching. Quickly her mind raced back to Morehouse College and Spelman College where she had sensed the risings in the souls of her black sisters and brothers. You could see it in Martin Luther King's eyes in those joint Sociology classes at Spelman and Morehouse. You could feel it in the air as the students went joyfully about their business.

Now, the march on Washington brought the expectation to a culmination. It was more than Clifton had dared to hope. The doubts and fears she had learned to accept as a part of life had dulled her ability to dream fully. The little traumas left by such things as having to go to the back doors of stores to get cokes in some Southern cities, the fear that she might get in the wrong places while traveling in the South, and the insults hurled by bigots, these and many more hurts had left their marks.

Actualizing the Dream

But, today when Martin Luther King, Jr. said, "I have a dream," Clifton could let her dreaming reach to new heights. She cried openly as he said, "All God's children will be free." Yes, thought Clifton, "It's *all* God's children. Not just the black or the brown children or the white children. We really are *all* God's children." The thought helped her to feel free to be her full self—black, white, brown, red, yellow and all the shades in between. It felt good to be human—fully human.

As the speech ended, Clifton thought about the various roads which led to this beautiful time. There were the loving parents who made her feel special in numerous ways. She was especially thankful for her father, who worked long and hard to get his Bachelor of Arts degree at the University of Iowa. He had to struggle for money to pay his tuition, but he made it! Her dad refused to stop growing, so after his four children were born he worked on his Master's degree at Kansas State University. She gloried once more in his marvelous example. He had claimed a dream. He claimed it even before Martin Luther King, Jr. articulated it for the whole black community.

Clifton rocked back in laughter as she reflected on the high school days where her dad was her strict and demanding Chemistry teacher. She made straight A's in all her subjects. School was easy for her but she really *earned* her A's in Chemistry. Her dad saw to it that she worked for her grades. What a fine model her father had been! He taught that hard work was the ticket to a good life.

Clifton thought of her mother. She was something special. She loved her kids and told them so. She challenged their minds by posing and solving arithmetic problems the kids couldn't decipher. Most of all she made life joyful. Sure, they didn't have much money but they had fun. They celebrated each other.

Having good parents was a marvelous blessing. Clifton was doubly blessed in also having other relatives who were using their lives constructively. There were two uncles who were physicians, one uncle was a college president, and another uncle was a domestic relations judge in New York City. Thus, Clifton could see many avenues black people might use to fulfill themselves. Sure, there were insults and problems, but Clifton also knew there were joys, and that life was good.

Spelman College was a special challenge for Clifton: she entered it when she was 15 years old. Here she was at this famed institution after making straight A's in high school. There were lots of boys, girls and fun things to do. The question was whether or not Clifton would take advantage of her many opportunities. After four years of fun and study she graduated with her bachelor's degree in Sociology. Along the way Clifton was elected to several academic honorary groups. The straight A high school student had climbed the steps toward her fulfillment.

After Spelman College, Clifton enrolled in New York University. Again, as a 19 year old student, Clifton was the youngest in her class. The days in New York gave her an opportunity to see Harlem and other black ghettos. She saw both the joy and the pain of black life in northern cities. Also, Clifton saw the excitement of young, black scholars at universities such as NYU, Columbia, Boston University and CCNY. She heard about Martin Luther King, Jr. from her sister at Columbia University. Clifton, like other young blacks, knew that things were happening to blacks' psyche. The joys of her childhood were being nurtured by the burgeoning growth of young black adults around her.

A 20 year old college graduate often has difficulty getting adults to take her seriously for responsible employment and Clifton was no exception. So, she did what Thomas Wolfe said she couldn't do and returned home. She brought with her a vision of education and humanity. Clifton knew that all people could live together in productive peace. The question was where and how to make her part of the dream come true.

The local school district needed a visiting teacher, so Clifton went to work in that capacity. For many years Clifton served the community as a visiting teacher. In this role she tried to see that children's needs were met. For some, it meant finding food and clothes. For some, it meant helping their parents find the proper agency to meet their needs. For others it meant teaching both parents and children the academic fundamentals. Always the task was bringing people together so they could help each other. Clifton's vision of people helping each other regardless of race was coming true every day.

The need for visiting teachers grew, and Clifton became the leader of an expanded group of colleagues. Her influence increased geometrically. Finally, as president of the state's visiting teacher association, Clifton led that group to an understanding that their task was to bring people together. As the main speaker at their annual banquet, Clifton spoke of the love of all mankind. The members stood unanimously in tearful but joyful applause.

Other challenges rose to meet Clifton, who completed her Ph.D. degree at a large woman's university where she was the first black student to attain that degree. Again, Clifton had blazed a trail. She wondered if she was claiming the dream that her father had seized. She pondered the surges of her soul she had felt at Spelman and NYU which had led her to

Actualizing the Dream

this day. At a deeper level, she knew she was fulfilling the humanity that her parents, uncles, aunts, brothers, sisters, and professors had affirmed throughout the years. As she and Troy, her husband, danced with joy they also paused to be thankful to all who had facilitated their growth.

Her Ph.D. degree and excellent work record helped to open the door to a position with a community college. Clifton was to have the joy of being a part of the staff which opened the college. At this institution she saw both students and staff grow and develop into better people. She felt like a midwife as she helped the people around her make constructive changes in their lives. Surely, this too was a part of the dream. The fires of Spelman and Morehouse and NYU were spreading. Clifton knew from first-hand experience that people could grow. She *knew* that blacks, browns, whites, reds and yellows could live in productive harmony.

Clifton's giving to others was returned to her in many ways. The staff selected her to represent them at a conference in Maine, where a group gathered to produce a book about junior colleges. Thus, Clifton met with thirty representatives from across the nation. Now she was a distinguished senior member of her profession. The laughing, dancing little girl was still alive within her, but it was complimented by the committed, competent woman who tried to facilitate others.

Her alma mater saw Clifton's potential and two years after her graduation invited her to join its staff. Clifton became another pioneer. She was the university's first black, female professor. Surely this was a peak, but there was more to come.

As Clifton went about her teaching assignments both the students and staff saw her special talents and skills. Enrollments in her classes became so large she had to limit them. Students of all races sought her for counseling and guidance. Many students chose to major in guidance and counseling because of her influence in their lives. The staff sought her counsel. Soon, people forgot that she was black. Clifton became a "real" person to the most bigoted of her colleagues. She soon became chairperson of her department.

Throughout her life Clifton had been joyful. She was glad to be alive. This always was evident in her poetry and music. As her maturity increased, Clifton became acutely aware of the good things in her life, and she compiled a book of her poetry. She called it *Melodies of Blackness* because she wanted to describe the joys of the black experience. Clifton knew of the pain of many black people, but she also knew of the joys of life. Her book reflected primarily on the day-to-day happenings which sometimes seemed so small and insignificant. Her book was her own song and one of her favorite poems is *A Song of Darkness*.

A Song of Darkness

I'm excited to be
Black and me.
Free of spirit and free from hate,
Filled with love and nourished by faith.

I'm happy to be
Black and free,
With nothing to change and little to protest,
I might have been dead and accomplished less.

It's fun to be
Black and me,
Loving and knowing all colors
Of my American sisters and brothers.

I'm grateful to be
Black and me,
With a heritage rich in history
Of art, music and spontaneity.

It's sad to be
Black and free,
And cry when I see some
Who have yet to overcome.

Be glad to be
Any color, but free.
Celebrate your life and individuality.
Rejoice in the excitement of diversity.

Thank you, that I am able to see
Beauty in the spectrum of humanity.
God, it's good to be me,
Black and free.

Even though she loved her poetry, Clifton became increasingly aware that success in life was at least partially attributable to systematic skills. Up to this time, Clifton had been fully committed to the poetic side

Actualizing the Dream

of her life. She appreciated the mystery in herself as she "magically" reeled off her poems. It seemed that this same magic accounted for much of her success in counseling. Clifton valued the "soul" in all people and she did not want to violate it. Yet she stayed open to new experiences.

Clifton watched various counselors delineate human skills which could be used with any human being in any setting. She saw the common sense in concepts such as good physical, emotional, and intellectual health. These skills were applicable to her students, her clients, her friends as well as herself. Also, Clifton saw that these areas could be subdivided into skills. She struggled with skills and always reminded others that it was humanity which counted the most.

Clifton began to teach skills in her classes. First, she taught people to attend to their client and then she included other skills such as responding empathically. Clifton opened herself to trying this systematic approach to helping people. At first, it seemed mechanical, but as she continued to use it, she saw that she had been using the skills all the time. The only difference was that now she could teach them systematically to her students. In a sense Clifton had found a way to integrate the process of her right brain lobe with those of the left lobe. Clifton understood that her intellectual skills helped her communicate her deepest feelings just as she created her poetry.

Clifton created with her skills. She systematically included poetry in her teaching; she systematically taught her students to use their own poetic responses in their counseling. Thus, Clifton had transitioned from being a person who thought that she needed to protect her uniqueness into a person who could explore it and thus share her personal learnings with others. Clifton had struggled successfully to use skills to express her humanity. As a result of her fine teaching, Clifton's students nominated her for the outstanding teacher award at her university which she won. Thus, Clifton was recognized by her students, colleagues, and administrators as one of the best teachers.

Peak experiences frequently are followed by valleys that develop other dimensions of our humanity. Clifton received a call from her younger sister in Atlanta, who related how the doctors had told her she had brain cancer. Clifton went immediately to be with her. The disease seemed to be moderate and Clifton returned home. As the cancer developed, Clifton made periodic trips to be with her sister. During each visit her hope was that if her sister could not conquer the cancer at least she would be able to live each day as fully as possible. Her sister continued to fail and Clifton's sadness was nearly unbearable. Still, she continued to visit and do her best to brighten her sister's last days.

Clifton Sparks

On what proved to be her final trip, Clifton had a fine visit with her sister. They spoke of pleasant things and they both felt vital. It was as if life came back to her sister. Clifton left feeling lifted and hopeful, but when she arrived at home she learned that her sister had died. Clifton's grief was crushing. She staggered under the blow. As she struggled to share her suffering with her family Clifton came to understand that it was wonderful to have had her sister for over forty years. She recalled that her own life was dedicated to living and that it must remain so. Perhaps her commitment to life deepened after her sister died.

When her sister died, Clifton thought about her father's death just two years earlier. Clifton recalled how she had held his hand tenderly not long before he died and she tried to be as fully human as possible. She hadn't known how many moments they would have. Clifton wanted to ask her father to live longer, but that was up to him. She strove to live fully in the moments they had.

Clifton's father had died while she was not with him. She arrived shortly after his death and remembered holding his hand as she had done many times while he was alive. It felt very much the same as when he was living. It was still the strong yet tender hand she had come to love. It was still the hand that had taught her so much about life and living.

Clifton wondered if death is a part of life. It seemed that death overcame life. But she came to know that when life is invested in life it grows and continues. An invested life becomes a part of the stream of humankind's constructive movement. No part can exist without the others. Clifton hoped she could see the whole building of humankind while still being a part of it.

Her sister's smile and her father's hands were lessons about life for Clifton. The sadness of Clifton's loss and the beauty of their lives taught her concretely that life is precious. The joy of a smile became a memory which guided her in times of pleasure. Clifton saw the balance of the lessons of life and vowed to give them to her students.

Clifton needed these lessons about life when she too faced serious surgery after which many questions remained. Clifton had to decide whether or not to live fully or retreat into self-pity. Essentially, she faced the question of whether or not her teachings were for real. She had told others that life was a privilege to live to its fullest.

Clifton chose to live as fully as possible. She had been made dean of the college of education prior to her surgery. She decided to plunge into her work. At first there were painful physical limits but as time passed she gained strength. In short, she affirmed her mission of teaching others by living her own life as fully as possible.

Actualizing the Dream

There's a song which says, "the road is long, with many a winding turn that leads to who knows where, who knows when." That describes Clifton Sparks' life. Still, there is a "thread that has run so true" through her life and that thread is to give others what she has learned about life. Clifton has passed along happy as well as sad lessons. The overarching theme has been that life is precious, not fragile, but exquisitely precious.

Clifton Sparks is a member of a profession, the teaching profession. She has joined hands with her colleagues and students as a part of humankind's march to fulfillment. Clifton has seen her students grow. She has seen her colleagues grow. She has seen tragedy and beauty. Most of all she has seen life and faced it squarely. Her forum has been the classroom and her instrument has been herself. Clifton's mission is a part of the dream of Martin Luther King, Jr. Clifton has looked down the long corridor of human history and taken her place among the people who try to help others. Clifton is a winner. She has strong credentials for any field of endeavor. Many people are happy that she chose education and because of her choice she touched their lives in a constructive way. Clifton belongs among the best and the brightest teachers.

Epilogue

Clifton's teaching effectiveness can be assessed directly and objectively. Her personal levels of functioning and teaching effectiveness are summarized on Chart 1.

Clifton has undergone serious medical treatment which has limited her physical functioning, but she has initiated a systematic physical program which will allow her to progress to Level 5. Perhaps, the emotional area is Clifton's main strength, particularly her mission. She has maintained her sense of professional direction for over 30 years. In the intellectual area, Clifton is in transition. She is a poet and for many years her systematic skills were somewhat bound by the structure of poetic thinking. Now, she is integrating poetic thinking with more systematic cognitive procedures which recently included enrolling in a computer science course.

Clifton's teaching demonstrates her superior levels of skills. Her trend toward more inclusion of systematic thinking is reflected in both her content development and her teaching delivery. As she becomes more systematic, she may develop and use the skills step requisite for Level 5.

Clifton typifies the growing teacher who is making the transition successfully into the Information Age. She has learned that a teacher can be both a poet and a systematic instructor. For some teachers, this will mean a development of interpersonal sensitivity. For others, like Clifton, it will involve learning and using systematic procedures. Clifton's triumph is that she is learning to combine the poetic with the systematic.

CHART 1
Effectiveness Chart for Clifton Sparks

Dimensions of *Personal Effectiveness*

PHYSICAL	5–Stamina	4–Intensity	3–Adaptability	2–Nonadaptive	1–Sick
EMOTIONAL					
Motivation	⑤–Mission	4–Self-fulfilling	3–Achievement	2–Incentive	1–Nonincentive
Interpersonal	⑤–Initiating	4–Personalizing	3–Responding	2–Attending	1–Nonattending
INTELLECTUAL					
Learning	⑤–Acting	4–Understanding	3–Exploring	2–Involvement	1–Noninvolvement
Substance	⑤–Technologizing	4–Operationalizing	3–Principles	2–Concepts	1–Facts
Teaching	5–Individual-izing	④.5	4–Goal-Setting	3–Diagnosing	2–Content	1–Unprepared

Dimensions of *Teaching Effectiveness*

Content Development	5–Skills Steps	④–Skills Objective	3–Principles	2–Concepts	1–Facts
Lesson Planning	⑤–Summarize Skill Steps	4–Exercise Skill Steps	3–Present Skill Steps	2–Overview Applications	1–Review Contingency Skills
Teaching Methods	⑤–Tell Show Do Repeat Apply	4–Tell Show Do Repeat	3–Tell Show Do	2–Tell Show	1–Tell
Teaching Delivery	5–Monitoring	④–Programming	3–Goal-Setting	2–Diagnosing	1–Preparing Content
Interpersonal Skills	⑤–Reinforcing	4–Individual-izing	3–Personalizing	2–Responding	1–Attending

2 / Sustaining the Promise

John McFarland

John McFarland stands six feet, four inches tall. When he puts on his orange Stetson hat with its University of Texas emblem, he seems seven feet tall. His eyes seem to pierce the space around him. John's voice is as loud and deep as a Metropolitan bass, yet he is as friendly and kind as our mutual images of our grandfathers. His course in life has been steady and true. He has spent his life as a student's advocate. That is his mission.

Most Texans are "A-Mur'-i-cans." They love this nation and the blood of many Texans has been spilled in our country's wars. John McFarland is Texan from head to foot, so what greater joy could he have had as a seventh grader than to accept an award from the mayor of Galveston on the Fourth of July. The reward was given to John for making the highest score on an American history test administered to all school children in Galveston, Texas. After receiving the award, this tall, lean seventh grader spoke to the audience about his love for America. His eyes must have sparkled as he felt a kinship with everyone present. John savored his feelings and has nourished them throughout his life.

Sustaining the Promise

John's academic progress continued as he excelled in all of his subjects. In fact, he did so well that he was salutatorian of his high school graduating class. In order to maintain his personal balance, John served his beloved Ball High School as business manager for the school's publications. The tall, young Texan could see a long way physically and intellectually, and he had many hopes for the future. At the conclusion of high school, John reflected on the people who had influenced his life profoundly. His sister had taught him to read before he entered the first grade. John was so precocious that he skipped the first and second grades and thus started his formal schooling in the third grade. His fourth grade teacher drilled him in arithmetic fundamentals. She taught him respect for academic discipline. There were so many fine people who had given him so much, and John felt humbly grateful to all of them.

John McFarland can say "Beat Hell out of Oklahoma!" louder than any one else, and he can be heard yelling this phrase at every Texas-Oklahoma game. He doesn't hate Oklahoma, he loves the University of Texas at Austin. He loves it because it has touched the depths of his soul. John earned his B.A. degree at U.T. with a major in government and minors in Latin and business. Again, John kept a broad view of life by serving in social groups on campus. He was manager of the baseball team, sports editor of the *Daily Texan* as well as the yearbook, and house manager of the Sigma Alpha Epsilon fraternity. Big John was active both academically and socially. He was alive and living. U.T. was a great place to be.

Tough times came to John after graduating from U.T. Jobs were scarce, so he found himself driving a truck prior to becoming a substitute teacher. Finally, John was hired as a regular teacher in Galveston. He taught geography in the fourth, fifth and sixth grades. John worked hard and things went well until one day when everything went wrong and John was so discouraged that he sent a letter of resignation to his principal. It was never mentioned. John learned patience and understanding in that experience.

John was invited to return to Ball High School to teach math. It was like going home and he worked harder than ever. He was happy. It was almost overwhelming when his colleagues asked him to be chairman of the math department. John loved his work and he felt he was giving something back to the school which had nourished him. To John, it was a beautiful love affair.

John's work at Ball High School was interrupted by World War II. After the usual basic training, John was administered a special test in mathematics. His score qualified him for special duty, so he was sent to

John McFarland

Cambridge, Massachusetts, where he trained at both MIT and Harvard. The training was related to the development of radar which involved some of the nation's greatest scientists. One of his joys was to be a part of the first group to use a large computer.

In spite of being very busy with his training, John found time to expand his cultural horizons. He fell in love with the Boston Symphony and its conductor Serge Kousevitsky. The whole setting at Cambridge seized John and he began to expand his world in all directions. John read from the great philosophers. He consumed reams of poetry. He devoured novels. After searching for a way to understand how the world had become so tangled in such an awful war, John decided to put his faith in the Bible. He believed that the Bible made more sense of life than any other book. The Bible has been his most important source of personal strength ever since that time.

When he left the Army, John returned to Ball High School as vice-principal. About half of the teachers there had taught John while he was a student at Ball High. When John became principal, it seemed like a dream come true. He worked harder than ever to help educate the students of his beloved school. At this time John came to understand that he had to be very organized in order to help others learn the skills necessary for a productive life.

Since he needed certification by the State Department of Education, John enrolled at the University of Texas for his Master's Degree. Again, he met people who impacted his life; Dr. J.G. Umstattd exemplified being a gentleman and a research scholar, and Dr. I.I. Nelson was a model of effective administration. While earning his Ed.D. in educational administration, it became clear to him that substantive material had to be explicated clearly for it to be delivered effectively to students. Thus, for his dissertation, John studied Life Adjustment Education, which explained the specifics of education for effective living. In this process, he was clarifying the skills necessary for substantive delivery to students. His training in mathematics skills was increasingly valuable to him. John came to understand that good intentions had to be implemented through well-organized delivery programs.

Many leadership opportunities opened for John. His solid voice, his training and his commitment made him a forceful spokesman for education across Texas. John coordinated student teaching at U.T. and spoke at meetings all over the state. His influence was growing.

It wasn't long before John was called to Vernon, Texas as superintendent. For four years, he led the system in a campaign to help students accept responsibility for their learning. As his fame spread, other systems

Sustaining the Promise

sought his services. Soon he went to Amarillo as superintendent. John recalled how they started a vocabulary skills class in Amarillo and saw a 20% gain in their SAT scores. These were great days, and John traveled far and wide to carry the message of education. He knew the answer to effective education lay in the work of well-intentioned teachers who utilized skills to accomplish their goals. John took his message to anyone who would listen. The tall Texan with the big voice, the fine mind and the big heart was giving all he had to the people he loved.

Texas faced the integration crisis with all of its problems like many other southern states. The big difficulties called for big people and John McFarland was called to Texas' largest city, Houston. As superintendent of Houston's schools, John was in the middle of the state's biggest crisis. Big John appeared at meetings too numerous to mention as he guided Houston through the integration crisis. The school board's meetings were televised, so many thousands of people saw John negotiate with the Board of Education for better learning for students. There was no place to hide. John's effectiveness, as well as that of hundreds of other people, depended literally upon his ability to maintain his sense of balance. Fortunately, throughout eight years of strife, there were no scenes of violence.

How did John maintain his sense of balance in Houston? John explained that it was a gift from God. He started each day (before 6 a.m.) with a prayer on his knees. He met regularly with some long-term friends. He stayed in touch with all groups by visiting each of Houston's 252 schools every year. He didn't take sides. He believed in people, all of them.

John had one secret way to cope with the board meetings. Before each meeting, he went to the YMCA for a massage, a steam bath, and a shave. After his massage, John would eat a bowl of soup and would arrive for the meeting, calm and cool.

At one point during the integration crisis, John was invited to address the state PTA convention. Having had a long standing affiliation with the PTA, John felt free to speak the truth as he saw it. So, he rose to his full stature and said, "We're reaping the harvest we have sown for so many years." The audience fell silent and John wasn't invited to address them again.

Happily, there were many good times during integration. One Houston teacher who had vowed to keep black children out of her school finally accepted a student body of 50% blacks. In fact, she led all her students and parents in singing, "Getting to Know You" when John visited her school. Although the struggle was tough, it was worthwhile and the tall Texan gloried at his chance to be a part of it.

John McFarland

John had learned to keep his life balanced; so throughout his superintendency in Houston he kept busy in community affairs. He was active on the boards of the Houston Symphony, Scouts, Y.M.C.A., United Way, Salvation Army, Red Cross, and he was president of the Houston Rotary Club, which is the world's largest of that kind. John listened intently to the professors at Rice University as well as to his own staff as they shared their insights and learning. Still, he believed that his fundamental strength was derived from his spiritual life. He continued to teach Sunday School classes as he had done throughout his adult life.

John continued to be a pillar of strength. He used his well-developed skills and fostered programs which delivered skills to students. John knew that theory alone was not sufficient for the crisis in Houston. Knowledge and understanding had to be delivered skillfully. He was so successful at his task that he was given the first award as most outstanding graduate of the University of Texas College of Education in 1963. Thus, U.T. had recognized its loyal son who had led Houston through desegregation while at the same time adding an average of 11,000 new students every year. Perhaps, the tensions generated by the integration crisis as well as the effects of many other struggles finally accumulated and John began to have some physical problems. The doctors advised John to take it easier so he assumed the deanship of the College of Education at the University of Texas at El Paso. Being an old war horse, John tore into his new job with the same old gusto.

The central theme of John's tenure at El Paso was the integration of people from Mexican and American cultures. This procedure brought out the usual cultural differences which were confronted in the training centers for Hispanic and American teachers. John rejoiced in the cultural difference and wanted to bring the teachers together in mutual respect. In order to accomplish a smooth integration of cultures, John employed systematic training skills which could be replicated in other settings. Because he trusted both his heart and his mind, he created skills programs which integrated empathic understanding with cognitive skills.

Opportunities come continuously to talented people and John was invited to Texas Woman's University as dean of the College of Education. He was touched by their invitation because T.W.U. is America's largest university for women. What a marvelous opportunity, particularly at the time when women's issues were being brought to the center of the nation's stage! John sensed that he would be where some important social action was taking place.

Sustaining the Promise

John understood that people who wish to be productive socially and politically as well as academically need to utilize their skills. At T.W.U., John put increased emphasis upon reading skills. He added reading experts to the faculty and employed as many reading specialists as possible. He became one of the initiators of the Right to Read Program for the state of Texas.

Additionally, he saw that education for gifted people, especially women, was being neglected. To meet this need, a program for gifted students was started. John focused that program upon both problem solving skills and cognitive skills because these were the abilities which were critical to gifted students. The skills were presented systematically to teachers of the gifted so that they could deliver them effectively to students.

John became increasingly convinced that it took both enthusiasm and substantive content to close the gap between people's hopes and their realities. He focused his attention on using both enthusiasm and systematic content in his own teaching. Yes, John taught while serving as dean of the College of Education at T.W.U. In fact, he often carried more than the usual full time teaching assignment while administering the entire College of Education. As usual, John was on fire for education.

For a time, John was asked to serve as acting Vice President for Academic Affairs. Being "a good trooper," he accepted the assignment, but he continued to teach his classes where he focused more intently on cognitive skills. John had developed a series of 33 specific thinking strategies which could be taught to administrators who in turn could instruct teachers in their use. His mind glowed as he saw the potential in teaching people how to think.

John's rich academic experience at Ball High School, the University of Texas, Harvard, MIT, and a host of other learning institutions had created a lasting excitement about the capacities of the human mind. With his cognitive strategies, John knew how to feed the mind systematically. It thrilled John's soul.

John plans his lesson for optimum delivery to his students. For instance, when he teaches *conceptualization*, one of the 33 thinking strategies he had identified, he devises a specific plan for his teaching. A typical plan follows:

Course Title:	Educational Administration
Unit:	Planning
Topic:	Cognitive Processes
Task:	Thinking Effectively
Skill:	Conceptualizing

John McFarland

1. Form a mental image of a curriculum for a specific class visualizing how students will react
2. Construct a diagram of the curriculum
3. Write the major divisions of the curriculum

In this manner John has concretized his ideas into specific skills which can be taught to his students. He is achieving a success rate of nearly 100%. That is, nearly all of his students learn to use the thinking strategies. John knows how to foster thinking among his students. His goal is to increase the number of administrators, teachers, and students who think analytically, logically, and wisely.

When John's assignment as Vice President of Academic Affairs ended, he returned to full-time teaching. Now he was free to focus on cognitive skills. Quickly he assumed responsibility for many dissertations and has been chairperson for 34 of them.

John also met a personal challenge while at T.W.U. He developed cancer and as usual, when faced with a challenge, John viewed his malady as a learning experience. It was humbling. It was frightening. It was distracting. It was painful. But, to John, it was not as powerful as God, and he had put his life in God's hands a long time ago. So, cancer, like ignorance and other forms of pestilence, was to be fought systematically within God's will. Thus, John continued his normal duties while undergoing the traumas of chemotherapy which he later described as a "cruel master." Fortunately, John seems to be free from his cancer. Now he calls his life "lagniappe" which means serendipity.

John McFarland is still six feet and four inches tall. He speaks loudly. He yells at University of Texas football games. He teaches with vigor. He prays every morning. He argues with his colleagues. He supports his colleagues. He is a student advocate. He is putting even greater vigor into his development of thinking strategies and problem solving. He uses computers in his research work. He is writing a book.

When John was asked about some of the high points of his teaching career, he seemed to turn and look down a long road. He ran his fingers through his full head of hair and smiled. You could tell that his view was good. John enjoyed what he saw. Then, he turned and said, "I've had my successes and my failures, some awful failures. But, I have always enjoyed teaching. I enjoy it now. I can hardly wait to get to class."

John is a winner. Obviously, he is talented. He has received more awards than most people dream of. Yet, his most ennobling statement is that he may have had more profound effects on humanity when he taught

Sustaining the Promise

geography to fourth graders than in all of his efforts as an administrator.

John is a teacher through and through. He has continually developed skills so that he could deliver them compassionately to human beings in whom he believes. John sums it up by saying, "It is all in the Master's hands. I just have fun seeing how He does His work. Meanwhile, I try to keep on being a student advocate, which is my mission."

Epilogue

John's personal effectiveness is assessed, as indicated on Chart 2. John's level of physical functioning is limited by some medical problems but as an old "warhorse" he transcends these problems in many instances. Without question, John is "super" high in the emotional area. His mission is clear and he charges the atmosphere with positive attitudes. In the intellectual area, John is making the transition to more systematic teaching processes. Earlier in his career, John preferred "big pictures" to more detailed ones, but at this time, he is devoting greater attention to the "nitty-gritty" steps of skills development.

John is a superior teacher whose personal development of a skills-step approach is reflected in his classroom teaching. As he acquires proficiency with these skills, he will apply them to his content development as well as his teaching delivery.

John's extended experience in education has whetted his appetite for more knowledge and better ways to transmit it to his students. His development of a taxonomy of cognitive strategies is his cutting edge as he moves into the Information Age.

CHART 2
Effectiveness Chart for John McFarland

Dimensions of Personal Effectiveness

PHYSICAL	5–Stamina	4–Intensity	3–Adaptability	2–Nonadaptive	1–Sick
EMOTIONAL					
Motivation	5–Mission	4–Self-fulfilling	3–Achievement	2–Incentive	1–Nonincentive
Interpersonal	5–Initiating	4–Personalizing	3–Responding	2–Attending	1–Nonattending
INTELLECTUAL					
Learning	5–Acting	4–Understanding	3–Exploring	2–Involvement	1–Noninvolvement
Substance	5–Technologizing	4–Operationalizing	3–Principles	2–Concepts	1–Facts
Teaching	5–Individualizing	4.5 / 4–Goal-Setting	3–Diagnosing	2–Content	1–Unprepared

Dimensions of Teaching Effectiveness

Content Development	5–Skills Steps	4–Skills Objective	3–Principles	2–Concepts	1–Facts
Lesson Planning	5–Summarize Skill Steps	4–Exercise Skill Steps	3–Present Skill Steps	2–Overview Applications	1–Review Contingency Skills
Teaching Methods	5–Tell Show Do Repeat Apply	4–Tell Show Do Repeat	3–Tell Show Do	2–Tell Show	1–Tell
Teaching Delivery	5–Monitoring	4–Programming	3–Goal-Setting	2–Diagnosing	1–Preparing Content
Interpersonal Skills	5–Reinforcing	4–Individualizing	3–Personalizing	2–Responding	1–Attending

3 / Crossing Boundaries

Marisa Valderas

Generalissimo Franco of Spain was hardly the person to foster democratic thinking in others. Strangely, he indelibly impressed freedom and independence upon the mind of Marisa Valderas. As a little girl in Spain, Marisa saw the hopelessness of the people around her and she decided to struggle always to be free and independent. The third child in a family of fourteen children, Marisa saw her parents struggle with adversity in order to feed and clothe the family. At her deepest level she felt keenly the resignation of her family and friends. The culture was stifling all of them and Marisa could not understand why they just accepted their fate. She vowed she would never do so.

In Marisa's family it was common for the older children to parent the younger ones so at the age of eight she was given a little brother to raise. She gladly accepted her challenge and gave her younger brother all the love she could. As she tried to help him grow, she realized that the environment lacked many things he would need to develop healthfully. There were no schools for her brother to attend, and Marisa feared that he would not learn the skills he needed. So, she took her brother to many

Crossing Boundaries

boarding schools trying to get them to give him a scholarship. Sometimes she was successful, but many times they refused. Marisa fought fiercely to see that her brother could live fully.

Marisa knew that she, too, would need an education, but there was no place to go. Almost in desperation Marisa begged her father, an accountant, to teach her Arithmetic. As he unfolded the secrets of mathematics she could see some of the elegant order of the universe. Marisa savored the time with her father as well as the joys of learning. For Marisa, skills held the keys to fulfilling her life. She searched for skills constantly, and seeking skills, Marisa was shaking her strong, little fist at ignorance.

Marisa soon learned that many things can be explained by cause and effect relationships. Those around her thought that life was ruled by caprice, but Marisa observed how things took place and she made predictions which came true. The more accurate her predictions, the more people thought of her as a mysterious person. They called her the "little witch." Marisa tried to tell them that she only kept track of how many things followed others in sequence, but her family and friends still thought of her as odd. Marisa was told that she thought too much. She often cried because she could not attend school. She wanted to think even more. Marisa was battling the people who did not want her to use her fine mind.

When she became 18 years old, Marisa persuaded one of the boarding schools to give her a scholarship. For the first time Marisa enrolled in a formal school. It was exciting! She could ask questions and get answers. Most of all, Marisa demanded skills that worked. Having been skeptical of easy ways to solve problems, Marisa knew that things had to work in the real world before they were of value to her. Soon she had conquered the skills offered by the school and began to look for new horizons. Marisa's educational quest had been short but it was typical of her approach to learning. She demanded the school's best and she gave her finest efforts.

Marisa lived her life intently and worried too much. She tried to solve other people's problems but many times she just could not do so. Life was hard and Marisa became more and more tense until one day while sitting at home she collapsed and nearly died. Her heart beat irregularly; for many weeks she was quite ill. From this experience, Marisa learned that she had to decide whether or not to let life overwhelm her. She found that she had real limits, and even though she wanted to make things right for others, she had to live within her own body. Marisa made a conscious decision to be healthy. So, for the next few months she concentrated on physical skills which helped her regain her physical strength. It was long and tedious but finally her physical health returned. Again,

Marisa Valderas

Marisa won her battle against the forces that would destroy her. She always remembered that she began to recover when she decided that she was going to fight with all her might against the illness that threatened her existence. Marisa continued to wage her conflict against all the things which tried to keep her from fulfilling her potential. This struggle had become her lifestyle.

Marisa's quest for learning had led down many non-traditional streets. Perhaps the most unusual path was her affinity for older people. She found them wise and willing to share their wisdom. It was as if they wanted to give their learning to anyone who would listen. Marisa sought all the older people she could find and spent many hours just exploring their worlds. This search led to one of her best friends, a ninety-six year old man who composed music. They shared endless hours as the older man gave Marisa his wisdom effortlessly and freely. The ease of the friendship was remarkable. Their souls seemed to touch; they understood each other intuitively.

Marisa and her composer friend both knew she had to seek broader horizons where she could expand her learning. Marisa told her friend that she would go anywhere, even to Hell, if she could learn. She confessed that her deepest fear was that she would someday suddenly stop learning or even wanting to learn.

When she was 20 years old Marisa decided to go to America to join her sister. The parting with her old friend was sad, but he gave her just one admonition—don't drink too much because American women tend to abuse their alcoholic consumption. Marisa promised him she would not drink in America and has kept that vow for eighteen years.

Marisa found America exciting and alive with learning. She also met a young attorney who seemed to be doing some important things with his life. The attorney and Marisa were so attracted to each other that six weeks after she arrived in America they were married. Marisa declared to her husband that she still was as eager to learn as when she was a child. He promised to help her learn as much as he possibly could.

After marriage, Marisa began to reflect even more systematically on her learnings because she wanted to pass her knowledge to her children. She recalled that Descartes, who was her hero, had taught her to practice her personal beliefs in herself by teaching her the statement "I think that I am, therefore, I am." Even before "meeting" Descartes she had known it was important to affirm her own existence. Everyday she tried to be sure that she listened to her internal voice more than those outside of her. She wanted to pass this wisdom to all the people she loved. Thus, as her children were born Marisa taught them to listen to themselves. She tried to give the same understanding to her brother and sisters in Spain. In fact, she traveled to Spain and brought them to America to give them this learning. In many ways this became a driving force in her life.

Before the first of her three children was born, Marisa conceptualized a picture of the best world they could have. She pieced it together from her own experience and the writings and teachings of everyone whom she thought had some important things to add to her understanding of childrearing. Marisa had decided that love is a crucial element of all human life so she introduced her children to people who could love them. Of course, some people criticized her for her childrearing practices, but she listened to her internal voice and kept taking her children with her to all her meetings. She remained undaunted.

Marisa soon found that she was conducting her most meaningful experiment in the way she was rearing her children. It soon was clear that she had no guarantees, because there were only risks in that business. Marisa refused to accept the concept of luck in her new experiment in childrearing and found that she had to rely on hard work, study and prayer. She believed that God did not determine the outcome of her work. He allowed her the freedom to succeed as well as fail. Marisa loved God and fought determinism as if it were her worst enemy. She fought deterministic thinking everywhere she found it. She gladly crushed determinism in herself as well as others.

Marisa expanded her childrearing skills and tried to teach her children many different skills—physical, intellectual, emotional, and spiritual. She kept her faith in people and wanted her children to know and love others.

Marisa is still experimenting in her childrearing. There are moments of doubt such as the time her daughter came to her and asked why Marisa had treated her children so importantly at home; when they were outside the home nobody treated them like they were important. Also, Marisa stands in awe of the influence of the peer culture. She wonders if the children's skills will be sufficient to the peer pressures of the teen-age culture. Marisa is grateful that things are going well for her children, but she also feels the vulnerability of all parents. She continues to rely on love, work, study, skills and God. Trusting is her greatest act of courage.

At the age of twenty-one, Marisa decided to extend her education formally by enrolling in the local community college. She had not mastered English very well, so college was a real challenge. Many people

Marisa Valderas

told Marisa "horror" stories about language requirements in college but she decided to conquer them just as she had determinism. Marisa slowly but surely acquired the necessary language skills and completed the community college curriculum. Not one to stop growing, Marisa reached deeper into herself and enrolled in the local university where she majored in Sociology because "she could inquire into people's lives without appearing to be nosy." Essentially, she wanted to expand her knowledge about people and sociology was her best vehicle.

In spite of the myriad of rumors about language difficulties Marisa graduated in 1976 with a B.A. in Sociology, having achieved a B average in her coursework. She had won the battle with the English language! It was very satisfying to graduate but by this time her mission had expanded and her "family" now included literally hundreds of people who had been less fortunate than she. Thus, when Marisa was offered a job as a social worker for the local school system she accepted. In a real sense, she accepted the challenge of eliminating some of the barriers which were keeping others enslaved.

As Marisa visited families of children who had various difficulties with the local schools, she learned more and more about life. She hated the forces of ignorance more and more. She discovered that the most important elements of her work were seeing the humanity in each of the people and giving them skills to solve their problems. Of course there were practical needs to be met such as food, shelter, and clothing but Marisa could see that even though these were sometimes crucial before problem solving could be initiated, it was essential to culminate her work with skills. If she did not deliver skills the people were apt to need more clothes or food immediately after the first intervention. Those skills had to be delivered in the context of deep personal respect for the recipients. Pity interfered. Marisa knew this deep in her soul and often reflected on her childhood in Spain where as a little girl she cried because she could not go to school. She knew that the "me" inside herself had turned into "we" as she joined her less fortunate friends in their struggle to go to school and she now included all the people she met. No longer was this a burden. It had become a glorious opportunity to be a part of humanity in quest for fulfillment.

Because of her informed caring, Marisa launched many projects among her Hispanic families. One of them was lessening absenteeism from school because it was higher among Hispanics than among other groups. Marisa began a skills training program to diminish the problem. Since Marisa believed in skills, she chose a generic skill to attack the

Crossing Boundaries

difficulty. It seemed to her that there were many problems involved in absenteeism. This meant that if she tried to solve just one of the problems there would still be literally hundreds of others left unsolved. On the other hand if she taught her people to solve problems, they could devise solutions to many of their own. Thus, she initiated a program of teaching problem solving skills to the children with the highest rates of absenteeism.

As the project unfolded, Marisa had to use many skills to keep the parents attending because they had some tough obstacles to overcome just to get to the training sessions. There were babysitting problems, transportation problems, scheduling problems . . . . The easiest path would have been to stop the effort, but Marisa kept remembering the little girl inside herself who cried because she could not go to school. She vowed not to let that happen to others. She also could see the value of the problem solving skills as the training sessions took place. So, she begged, borrowed and appropriated things to keep the training sessions going.

The group of parents met once a week for eight weeks. The learning goal for each parent was to be able to construct a problem solving matrix for a "real" life problem. Each session had a specific goal.

Session 1: Each parent could call the name of every other parent.
Session 2: Each parent could identify a specific real-life problem in their own lives.
Session 3: Each parent could accurately explain the problem solving matrix.
Session 4: Each parent could devise a list of five alternative solutions to their real-life problem identified in session 2.
Session 5: Each parent could specify their values which they used in the real-life problem identified in session 2.
Session 6: Each parent could rank order their values they specified in session 5.
Session 7: Each parent could complete the problem-solving matrix for the real-life problem identified in session 2.
Session 8: Each parent could successfully explain their problem-solving matrix for the real-life problem identified in session 2.

Marisa's criteria for success was that all (100%) of her parent-trainees successfully could complete the task for that session.

In order to accomplish her goal, each session was prepared in the step-by-step procedure. For example, the steps for the first session included the following:

Step 1: Marisa introduced herself.
Step 2: Each parent introduced himself or herself.
Step 3: Marisa made at least one interchangeable response to each parent as he or she was introduced.
Step 4: Each parent was asked to give some special clue which could help the group member remember his or her name.
Step 5: Each parent gave a special clue to remember his or her name.
Step 6: After each parent gave their special clue each member stated the name of all the members who had given their name. This proceeded until all members could name all the other members.

At the conclusion of the lesson the goal had been achieved. All members could name the other members.

Using this systematic approach, the group attained all training goals. Sometimes the members needed to modify the program in order to accomplish their goal. When this happened, Marisa used her program development skills to identify and implement the necessary changes.

When the training was completed, the results indicated that the parents had indeed learned the problem solving skills. It was a real world success for Marisa who took encouragement from Carkhuff who had devised the skills and she knew they would work in his real world. That had always been her test for skills. She knew it could happen.

Having succeeded in teaching the problem solving skills to the parents, Marisa wondered if the absenteeism among the children had decreased. She gathered data about the school attendance of the children whose parents had received the problem solving training. The results were clear. The students' absenteeism had been reduced significantly! Marisa had accomplished her goal through specific skills training. Surely she had been motivated, but also she had used a procedure that could be employed anywhere people desired to do so. Certainly, this was a vital part of a system which did not rely on luck or caprice. It was a way people could use to be more fully human. She knew it would work in Spain. In fact, she returned to Spain and taught it to some of the people in her home town.

Crossing Boundaries

Marisa has been involved in many projects designed to help people improve their lives. She has learned that the only projects which work across long periods of time are those which focus on skills. Marisa does not merely dream of solutions which will suddenly make the world a wonderful place. She knows that skilled people can say, "I am" because they can make things happen in their real world. In short, skills make people potent by allowing them to develop their potential and finally to experience the soul within them.

It is a long way from Spain to America, from illiteracy to literacy, and from not being able to go to school to being a teacher. It is a long way from wondering if people can improve their life through skills to a confirmed realization that they can. Marisa has covered the distance depicted by each of these statements. All the while she has been firm in her personal resolve to listen to the voice within her. She responds fully to other voices only when they call her to life. Then, she answers fully and joyfully with a smile that is full.

Marisa has had many reasons to give up. She also has many reasons to be cynical and selfish. But, Marisa stands firm and optimistic. She is also kind. Marisa declared unashamedly that she still cuddles her teenage children and that love is the most important thing in the world. Marisa literally shakes her fist at the world and says, "I think that I am, therefore I am." She is a battle-hardened veteran of educational wars who is integrating her Hispanic brothers and sisters into the mainstream of American Education. Marisa is among the best and the brightest teachers. That is quite a triumph for a woman who had to struggle very hard for both an education and her physical life. Perhaps her greatest victory is that she now helps others to seek life more abundantly.

Epilogue

Marisa's personal effectiveness is assessed as indicated in Chart 3. Marisa's physical stamina and her mission energize her to high levels of learning. The skills of systematic learning are relatively new to her so she is still mastering them. Her learning curve definitely is on the incline.

Marisa's teaching skills as summarized on the chart also indicate that she is a young and growing learner who is still acquiring the skills of systematic learning and teaching. Unlike her older colleagues who must unlearn ways of learning and teaching, Marisa can move directly to her task. This raises the issue of the rate at which people can make a transition into the Information Age. Apparently, keeping up with progress during the Information Age is as difficult as entering it and will require unlearning skills. Thus, perhaps Marisa as well as her older colleagues, indeed all of us, must learn to forget as well as to remember in the Information Age.

CHART 3
Effectiveness Chart for Marisa Valderas

Dimensions of Personal Effectiveness

PHYSICAL	⑤–Stamina	4–Intensity	3–Adaptability	2–Nonadaptive	1–Sick
EMOTIONAL					
Motivation	⑤–Mission	4–Self-fulling	3–Achievement	2–Incentive	1–Nonincentive
Interpersonal	⑤–Initiating	4–Personalizing	3–Responding	2–Attending	1–Nonattending
INTELLECTUAL					
Learning	⑤–Acting	4–Understanding	3–Exploring	2–Involvement	1–Noninvolvement
Substance	5–Technologizing	④–Operationalizing	3–Principles	2–Concepts	1–Facts
Teaching	5–Individualizing	④–Goal-Setting	3–Diagnosing	2–Content	1–Unprepared

Dimensions of Teaching Effectiveness

Content Development	5–Skills Steps	④–Skills Objective	3–Principles	2–Concepts	1–Facts
Lesson Planning	⑤–Summarize Skill Steps	4–Exercise Skill Steps	3–Present Skill Steps	2–Overview Applications	1–Review Contingency Skills
Teaching Methods	⑤–Tell Show Do Repeat Apply	4–Tell Show Do Repeat	3–Tell Show Do	2–Tell Show	1–Tell
Teaching Delivery	5–Monitoring	④–Programming	3–Goal-Setting	2–Diagnosing	1–Preparing Content
Interpersonal Skills	⑤–Reinforcing	4–Individualizing	3–Personalizing	2–Responding	1–Attending

4 / Implementing a Mission

Hila Pepmiller

In the West you can see a long way if you just take the opportunity to look. Hila is from the West and has looked a long way. In fact, Hila sees her life in eternal terms because she is sure that she and her students will live for eternity. This eternal vision of humanity guides her personal life as well as her teaching.

How did Hila come to see teaching in eternal terms? Well, Hila has lived most of her life with people who also believe in God. Her tall, handsome father wanted his special little girl to honor God and her mother's gentle touch reminded her of the very presence of the Almighty. Hila's parents treated her as if she were special and so she felt like a gift from God at an early age.

Hila's parents were very strong and they wanted her to develop her many physical talents. They moved from her birthplace to a small town when she was four years old. Hila recalled that she was lonely and depressed because she had no playmates. It was at this time that she taught her first class. She placed her dolls in circles and taught them

Implementing a Mission

lessons she was learning at Sunday School. Even at this very early age, Hila was certain that God wanted her to be a teacher.

It may seem that a little girl who is treated as something special by her father would become spoiled and protected. However, Hila was placed in a family leadership role because her older brother was often ill. She did farm chores just like her brothers. In fact, she was stronger than her brothers so she did more than they. Hila developed into a very healthy, strong and bright child. Her parents loved her development and focused it with stern discipline. She was nourished but she was expected to perform.

Hila's formal education began in a one-room school. Her teachers were Catholic sisters who were strict and rigid but loving. It was fun to compete with her older brother in subjects most students do not attempt until later in school. Things were pretty smooth except that Hila learned about devils, angels and God from the Sisters' catechism even though her father had warned her not to attend. She and her brother would hide in the ditch outside the school until catechism was completed. However, in the long run Hila was thankful the sisters had taught her that a person could be both academically thorough and biblically sound.

The years at the little school were good but her parents realized that the limited opportunities were retarding their children's learning, so they moved when Hila was 11 years old. The change to the larger school was drastic and Hila found that she was behind the others academically. She also was different from the others in her way of dress. Her farm-type clothes were out of date. On the other hand, Hila was pretty and as the tallest person in her class she was able to attract positive attention. Fortunately, her sixth grade teacher was a superb instructor who helped Hila close the academic distance between herself and the others.

Some good things happened to Hila during her Junior High days. A younger brother was born and Hila was able to help with the mothering. This was both good and bad because the new member of the family took some attention from Hila who occasionally pinched her brother to make him cry. When the crying started, her mother would take over the childrearing and Hila was free to play. The good part was that she had to expand her humanity to include the newcomer.

Hila's parents decided that their tall, strong, pretty, brown-eyed teen-age daughter who was quite athletic needed to develop some of her feminine skills so she enrolled in courses designed to teach the social graces. These skills were to serve her well late in life as well as during the transition from "tomboy" to womanhood.

Hila Pepmiller

The high school Hila attended was a laboratory school for a university, thus, many of Hila's teachers were college students. She gloried in her school life and participated enthusiastically in many activities. Hila was very active socially. She was a cheerleader and a member of the choir, as well as a star on the basketball team. Not surprisingly, she did not set any academic records though she did well in her courses, particularly English.

A most significant influence came into Hila's life during high school. She became convinced that God was giving her a special call to teach. She had always been active in her Christian life but she found her relationship to God greatly intensified. Hila prayed and read the Bible regularly, but most of all, she had felt a deep and profound relationship with Jesus Christ. She felt a need to get on with her work and finish high school in three years. Thus, at the age of 16 she was ready to enroll in college.

Deciding on a college was difficult for Hila who now loved people in a special way because she saw them as eternal creatures of God. Since her brother was enrolled at a private university in a large metropolitan area, Hila enrolled there. However, as the semester unfolded it became clear that Hila was not ready for the big city setting. So, after many tears, she returned to her hometown to enroll in the local university, where she majored in elementary education with minors in music and English.

College life offered a range of experiences which were to expand Hila's life space. She joined many organizations and was socially active. One of her highest moments was the day she was elected Homecoming Queen. She also was selected as a Sun Princess. Her life was full and active in many ways.

Conversely, Hila traveled through some valleys. An unmarried friend became pregnant, and Hila had to learn to accept her as a Christian sister even though Hila felt she had committed adultery. This was very difficult for a dedicated Christian. Hila grew to accept this situation and has remained very close to her roommate. Additionally, Hila fell in love with a football player who rejected her. It was her first experience with a broken heart. In her disillusionment, Hila tried to make her lover jealous and sometimes used other people to accomplish her ends.

Hila felt a need to expand her horizon so she traveled to the West Coast where for the first time she entered a bar. She was repulsed by what she saw. She felt a deep sorrow for the people who were harming their bodies, minds and souls with various drugs. It was as if someone were

Implementing a Mission

desecrating something sacred because, to Hila, the human being is a temple of God.

Throughout her college life Hila continued her prayer and worship. She felt herself moving closer to God and at times she thought she could see His influence in everyone. Hila was impressed particularly by the lives of the little children. She thought often of the biblical verses which said, "Suffer little children to come unto me and forbid them not, for of such as these is the Kingdom of God." Hila was so anxious to begin her teaching that she finished her program in 3 years. Thus, at the age of 19 she was ready to begin her teaching career. Hila was particularly grateful to Dr. Mitchell Jones, dean of the College of Education, who often encouraged her to continue to grow in all phases of her life.

Hila knew she was going to disappoint her big, strong father if she became a teacher because he wanted her to marry a rancher. Still, she chose teaching and started her first job in a small school with two other teachers. Hila lived alone in a small apartment and sold tickets at the local theater to supplement her tiny income of $200 per month. She was lonely but she loved teaching the bright little kids who attended her school.

Just as she had done as a student, Hila moved to a larger city to expand her horizons. She was assigned to teach a bilingual second-grade class of Mexican-American students. Hila visited their homes regularly and learned to respect their culture and strove diligently to show her love for each of them. Hila wanted her students to know their academic material and most of all she hoped they would know they were created in the image of God.

While teaching her beloved students Hila met "Mr. Right." He was a member of the Air Force who was also a devout Christian. They found that they had many things in common, such as dancing and singing. She loved his tender, mannerly ways of living and respected his intelligence as well as his strong religious faith. The 6'2" Air Force man won her heart and they were married after a six-month courtship. Her students were thrilled for their teacher.

Hila's marriage meant many changes in her life. For one thing it necessitated her leaving her hometown and going with her husband to his new place of employment in Iowa. Hila cried all the way to Iowa and wondered if she would ever be happy away from home. At first she did a variety of things to make ends meet for the family, and finally she got a steady job as a ninth grade teacher in the local school. Hila felt that at least a part of her was returning home, for the classroom was the place to which God had called her.

Hila Pepmiller

Hila moved to Missouri when integration was at its height and though it seemed strange to her, this was a difficult process. Hila's class was about 50% black and it seemed that her problems would be minimal. But, one day she returned to her classroom to find a little black boy who had painted his skin white so he wouldn't suffer any more for being black. She told him how much she loved him and how much God loved him. Hila felt her soul go out to this little boy as if she were enveloping him. She was making real contact, for even today she and this fine young man keep in touch with each other.

Hila reflected long and often on the little black boy who painted his hand white. She reminisced about her little hometown when she drove through "nigger" town with her family. She thought of the poverty of that place and of the pain of the people in it. Hila also thought about the songs she sang in Sunday School.

> "Jesus loves the little children
> All the children of the World
> Red and Yellow, Black and White
> They are precious in his sight
> Jesus loves the little children of the world."

It brought agony to her soul to think of how God must have suffered over the things that people were doing to His black children. Hila thanked God that He was expanding her soul to include her black brothers and sisters. She prayed that God would end all the prejudice soon.

Hila and her husband had been blessed with two fine, healthy daughters. The family was very close knit and Hila tried to teach her children everything she thought they might need to live effectively. Although she had known for a long time that skills were important, that reality was pressed more clearly into her mind every day with her children. Hila saw more clearly the souls in her own children. She was compelled to work harder and harder to help them feel their worth and develop the skills to live fully. Teaching children became her clear mission. And her choices became easier as she surrendered more fully to it.

Hila's husband was transferred to a large city, so the family moved to one of its suburbs. Hila decided to start a kindergarten where she could teach her true beliefs more fully. The school was sponsored by a church and Hila was the director for six exciting years. Of course there were various struggles to keep the school open, but in Hila's words, "God always met our needs." In this situation Hila learned the business world.

Implementing a Mission

She vividly recalled her learnings during a lawsuit brought by one of her parents. The "real" lesson for Hila was that she learned truly to forgive another person.

Hila was soon to be called to a larger ministry of teaching. One of the state universities was sponsoring a workshop for kindergarten teachers and selected Hila along with 25 others to begin a state-wide effort to establish kindergartens. This one-year program was exciting for Hila. She had time to develop learning programs which would help teachers deliver skills to students in a very caring way. She had known it was possible to do so and now she had helped develop the technology to help it happen. Surely, this work was a part of her mission.

After completing one-year of study Hila and her colleagues traveled across the state conducting workshops for kindergarten teachers. It was a wonderful experience to see the light in teachers' eyes as the group showed them the details of a kindergarten. To Hila it was comparable to how Michelangelo must have felt as he put together the tiny strokes of paint that finally became the ceiling of the Cistine Chapel. She recalled that at the outset of her year's study she had had a concept of how a kindergarten might be, but now she and her colleagues had the details. It was thrilling! It was always amazing to see the number of adults who really wanted to help kindergartners but who simply had no idea of how to conduct the program for these 5-year-old children. Hila felt like a midwife assisting these well meaning people in giving birth to their dream of a local kindergarten.

Hila's family had assumed a new direction during this time. They had adopted a little Indian boy who had been abused by his parents. At first they thought of the joys of this new addition but the reality was somewhat mixed. He wouldn't let Hila even touch him. He hid from people like a frightened animal. He was covered with boils and was hostile toward everyone. The family was pushed nearly to its limits of love and understanding as they tried to win the new brother and son to their hearts. Hila recalls that after many trying times she learned another lesson. She had to accept her son as he was. It was a new level of acceptance for Hila because it meant including some things she did not like at all. It meant saying it was okay for her son to be whatever he needed to be.

The struggle for their son and brother has been long and continuous. The progress of Hila's family is a testimony to the power of enlightened love.

Upon returning home Hila was asked by the local school board to start a kindergarten for the local public schools. She was to be the lead

lead teacher for the entire program. So, Hila and her staff began to develop specific learning programs for physical development, fine motor skills and language development. They focused on interpersonal skills which indicated to each child that he or she was a very special person. Thus, with her high motivation and her well-developed skills programs, Hila began her job as head teacher. Her guiding hand could be felt in all areas of the program and finally her impact was recognized by her colleagues who selected her as teacher of the year for the entire school system. Of course, Hila was pleased but she continued to judge her success by the skills acquired by her students. In her assessment of skills Hila placed high priority upon both the students' feeling of self worth and their academic progress. Thus, with skills and motivation Hila was fulfilling her mission.

By way of example, Hila planned her lessons so as to deliver the necessary skills to her students. The following lesson is typical of Hila's classroom teaching:

"Today, you will learn to use rulers to measure how long things are," Hila said as she passed out shiny new rulers and a laboratory ditto to each learner. Directing their attention to a large cardboard model which duplicated the markings on their rulers, she asked, "What do these large markings with the numbers mean?"

"Inches! Yeah, that's right! One inch, two inches. . . " Several learners in the class responded to Hila's question.

"That's right, Sue! Good, Tony! These marks do stand for inches," Hila said. Then she held up a chalkboard eraser and a ruler. She told the students the steps she was taking to measure the eraser. "First, put the end of the ruler with the 'one,' at one end of what you want to measure. Then follow along the ruler until you come to the end of what you want to measure. Can you tell the class how long this is, Tom? Six inches is the right answer!"

Next, the class used their rulers to measure the length of the lab ditto and write this figure on a piece of scrap paper. She circulated to check their answers. Dividing the class into groups of four, she assigned them to different lab stations. Here the learners received additional practice measuring pre-selected items. Later in the day, Hila had pairs of learners measuring and cutting four-inch squares and triangles out of different colored construction paper. Then the children decorated the bulletin board with a geometric border made from their measured shapes. Through this kind of systematic teaching Hila translated her love into effective learning by the students.

Implementing a Mission

Hila was soon to learn other lessons. She contracted cancer and underwent surgery and chemotherapy treatment. The pain and anguish were awesome at times. However, Hila's major question was what God wanted her to learn. So, she prayed and "went with" the events while waiting for some sign of their meanings. Her colleagues and family offered loving support. Most of all Hila felt very close to God. It was as if God spoke to her in His tenderest tones.

Soon Hila's new direction became clear. She spent many hours with other patients helping them cope with their illness. This was fulfilling and well received by others. After a period of healing Hila joined a group called Reach-to-Recovery. Again, Hila learned more about the power of combining God's love with human effort. She could see the healthy impact of sustained, systematic helping.

While continuing her work as lead teacher in the kindergarten as well as with Reach-to-Recovery, Hila saw a need to teach parents how to relate more effectively to their children. So, true to her course, she began a training program for parents. The program focused on combining skills with love. They have met regularly and allow parents to share their problems with childrearing. The program works. Parents with training in childrearing are more effective than they would have been without it.

The tall, brown-eyed lady stands straight today. She has battled many of life's problems. Still, she says that through the grace of God she is able to do His will. Undaunted by the difficulties, she combines His love with the skills He teaches her. She presses on toward her mission. Her family is growing. Her students are learning. Her support group for cancer patients (Reach-to-Recovery) is flourishing. Her program for teaching parent effectiveness is indeed effective. Hila says, "I owe it all to God. I can only pray that I can help more people feel worthy in the sight of God and of men."

Recently, Hila held a little six month old girl in her arms while she made marks on a blackboard. The little girl watched curiously and smiled a big, toothless grin. Hila hugged her warmly and her eyes filled with tears. Hila said, "Isn't God good to give us such wonderful people to share our lives." This is the spirit which motivates Hila. Her knowledge and skills about human growth and development are the substance she delivers so effectively. Her teaching is her skillful combination of her motivation and substantive content. It is an effective combination.

Hila is a winner. She belongs among the best and the brightest teachers because she delivers her content effectively to her students whether they are children or adults. Most of all, she teaches her students about the excitement of life and helps them to taste it in their own lives. May it ever be so.

Epilogue

Hila's personal and teaching effectiveness as assessed on Chart 4 are clearly superior in all areas. She brings into the forefront the role of spiritual strength in personal fulfillment. If this area were divided into skills such as prayer and worship, Hila would be at level 5 in each. She holds that this is the core of her life and gives God all the credit (praise) for her life.

Hila has conquered and used all the skills of a master teacher. She teaches with ease and zest and it seems that there is no limit to her productivity. She makes teaching look easy because she has mastered the skills it requires.

CHART 4
Effectiveness Chart for Hila Pepmiller

Dimensions of Personal Effectiveness

	5	4	3	2	1
PHYSICAL	5–Stamina	4–Intensity	3–Adaptability	2–Nonadaptive	1–Sick
EMOTIONAL					
Motivation	5–Mission	4–Self-fulfiling	3–Achievement	2–Incentive	1–Nonincentive
Interpersonal	5–Initiating	4–Personalizing	3–Responding	2–Attending	1–Nonattending
INTELLECTUAL					
Learning	5–Acting	4–Understanding	3–Exploring	2–Involvement	1–Noninvolvement
Substance	5–Technologizing	4–Operationalizing	3–Principles	2–Concepts	1–Facts
Teaching	5–Individualizing	4–Goal-Setting	3–Diagnosing	2–Content	1–Unprepared

Dimensions of Teaching Effectiveness

	5	4	3	2	1
Content Development	5–Skills Steps	4–Skills Objective	3–Principles	2–Concepts	1–Facts
Lesson Planning	5–Summarize Skill Steps	4–Exercise Skill Steps	3–Present Skill Steps	2–Overview Applications	1–Review Contingency Skills
Teaching Methods	5–Tell Show Do Repeat Apply	4–Tell Show Do Repeat	3–Tell Show Do	2–Tell Show	1–Tell
Teaching Delivery	5–Monitoring	4–Programming	3–Goal-Setting	2–Diagnosing	1–Preparing Content
Interpersonal Skills	5–Reinforcing	4–Individualizing	3–Personalizing	2–Responding	1–Attending

5 / Growing with the Team

Carl Tatum

Carl was born in a small Mississippi town. His father, Bill, was a logger in a sawmill camp where he made his living the hard way. Bill wanted to give Carl the best of everything but since money was in short supply he settled for giving him the best he could. Often the best he had to offer was a loving, strong hand. Still, he communicated love to Carl who felt that he was a very special dad. Carl pleasantly remembered the aroma of his dad's pipe. In fact he was quite certain that was one of the reasons he himself smoked a pipe almost incessantly as an adult.

Carl's mother was also special to him. Unfortunately, she died when Carl was only four years old, but in those few short years she left an indelible impression on him.

Sometimes Carl would tell of his wish that he could be hypnotized so he could remember his mother's words to him just before she died. It seemed to him that she had tried to tell him all the good things a person needs to know in order to live. Carl experienced a second loss when his dad died when he was eight years old. This event orphaned him legally, but Carl never considered himself an orphan.

Growing with the Team

When Carl finished high school he wanted to go to college but that seemed a distant dream. Fortunately, Carl's high school teacher knew some people at college on the West Coast so he and Carl traveled west to see about enrolling in that institution. Carl took the usual entrance tests and enrolled in special courses because his scores were too low for normal ones. For the first time Carl began to understand the importance of skills in his education. He vowed that he would learn the necessary skills to become a good student. Four years later Carl graduated with honors after having been placed in remedial English during his freshman year.

Carl's conviction about the importance of skills led him to teach them to his students in his sixth grade classes. It was clear to Carl that people needed two sets of skills—one to live effectively and another to learn efficiently. Carl searched for people and materials that would emphasize life skills and academic skills and wherever he found them he tried to incorporate them in his teaching. There were not many skills programs in either area, so Carl knew of the huge need to try to close the gap.

After teaching for five years Carl was asked to become the principal of an elementary school and so he began the second major area of his education career. He tried to lead teachers and parents into an emphasis upon both living skills and learning skills. Again, the lack of materials in both of these areas was painfully apparent. Miraculously, Carl heard Dan Prescott speak about Human Growth and Development and it seemed that his prayers were answered. Dan told of systematic ways to teach children and parents as well as teachers about the skills necessary to combine healthy lives with effective learning. Finally, Carl had met a person who kept his focus on the totality of the human being. He was tired of the segmented approaches of many experts. Carl was convinced that people could not be studied solely as portions of an entire organism. Also, he was profoundly dedicated to the notion that human beings were *not* determined to be self-destructive. Everything that he saw told him that people tried very hard to become the best persons they could be. Carl was saddened when he saw the struggle for healthful living blocked by circumstances. Thus, Carl embraced Dan Prescott and the Human Development movement.

Carl taught the skills developed by Dan Prescott's group wherever he could. He even enrolled in the doctorate program to improve his knowledge of skills. When he completed his doctorate he returned to his elementary school principalship where he continued his quest to teach the skills as far and wide as possible. Carl traveled to PTA meetings, taught summer school at various universities, and visited professional conferences to spread the word.

Carl Tatum

  Carl's opportunities to influence teachers grew as he joined the faculty of a major university where he taught the skills to hundreds of undergraduate and graduate students. Always Carl combined human skills with academic skills as he tried to focus on the gestalt of people.
  Because Carl could see the needs for more and better skills training procedures, he kept searching. Almost as if fate had led him, Carl met Robert Carkhuff, who was beginning a new and vital movement into the facilitation of people. Bob, too, was focusing on skills, so there was a sudden attraction between them. This meant a whole new start for Carl and he welcomed the opportunity.
  Equipped with specific skills training procedures produced by Carkhuff for the areas of interpersonal skills, physical fitness and substantive delivery, Carl began to look beyond his university students and began conducting workshops for practicing teachers as well. He traveled to Michigan, Florida, Tennessee, Louisiana, Washington, D.C., California and throughout Kentucky. In each workshop Carl tried to clarify the physical, intellectual and emotional skills needed for effective teaching. In Michigan, Carl saw major universities shift their emphasis to skills training. In Florida he helped a large school system conduct studies of teachers' skills. In D.C., he spoke with Abraham Maslow about human skills. In California Carl heard the world's experts discuss ways to upgrade academic skills. In Louisiana Carl taught teachers from around the state about physical, intellectual and emotional skills they could use in their classroom. During all this time, integration was a major issue and with his southern voice Carl could find the words to make integration more palatable to his fellow southerners. In short, Carl was using his skills as he talked about them.
  As he traveled across America teaching and demonstrating skills, Carl noticed that people who wanted to learn skills could be found in every town and city. In some places there was only one person, while in others there were many people, but collectively there was a large group throughout the nation and indeed the world. It occurred to Carl that if these people who wanted skills could be brought together they would constitute a strong group for positive human development. Carl knew there were other organizations which advocated humane teachings, but he also could see that no other group was advocating a skills approach to this topic.
  One day he heard some of his former students talking about a plan to bring together the people who wanted to use skills training to facilitate human development. Carl glowed as their plan unfolded. They had

Growing with the Team

devised a strategy which used audio and video tapes to transmit the training and to assess its effectiveness. Carl could see that even though these people from throughout the world could not be brought together physically, they could keep in touch with each other via video and audio tapes. They could share their new learnings and demonstrate for each other. It seemed to Carl as if the gordion knot had been cut. It was now possible to teach and learn skills for physical, intellectual, and emotional health to his fellow travelers even though they were miles apart.

Carl saw his former students master skills training programs as well as procedures for evaluating their effectiveness. He studied their work and applied it in workshops with teachers. It was hard for him to use the new human technology. It was different from some of his former approaches. But he learned it and used it.

Carl worked with his students in many of their studies and found that he was a very effective trainer. In one study in Miami, Florida, he trained teachers in the use of empathic understanding as part of their teaching strategy. Carl trained sixteen teachers for eight weeks and the results indicated that all sixteen of his trainees increased their use of empathic statements during their normal periods of classroom instruction. This outcome takes on a greater significance when compared to several other trainers who achieved significant increases by eight or less of their trainees. Carl was the star! He had entered a new age of skills development and he could use them effectively.

Carl's workshop for teachers was a success because he planned it systematically. The following weekly goals were established.

1st Week: Each teacher could discuss specific research about the efficiency of empathic understanding in the classroom.
2nd Week: Each teacher could identify an interchangeable statement from written, audio-recorded, video-recorded and live interaction between people.
3rd Week: Each teacher could make an interchangeable response to another person.
4th Week: Each teacher could make an interchangeable response to each member of a class of ten students.
5th Week: Each teacher could make an interchangeable statement to an entire class.
6th Week: Each teacher could make 3 interchangeable responses to an entire class of 25 students within a one-hour period of normal classroom instruction. That is, the

interchangeable responses were to be a part of normal classroom instruction.

7th Week: Each teacher could make at least 10 interchangeable responses during a one-hour period of normal classroom instruction.

8th Week: Each teacher could video record one-hour of normal classroom instruction and determine the number of interchangeable responses that had been made during that period.

There were goals for each day of the training procedure. For the first week the following daily goals were established:

Monday: Each teacher would be able to call each other's names as well as explain the goals of each person for the workshop.

Tuesday: Each teacher could define empathy and explain the skills of attending, observing, listening and responding.

Wednesday: Each teacher could explain research related to student's cognitive gains.

Thursday: Each teacher could explain research about the relationship between empathy and student attendance.

Friday: Each teacher could explain research about the relationship between empathy and student self-concept.

The success of Carl's work was further assured by his organization of each day's 2-hour lesson. For example, Wednesday's lesson for the first week was planned as follows.

Course title: Empathic understanding in the classroom.
Unit: Research related to empathy in the classroom.
Topic: Empathy and cognitive gains in the classroom.
Skill: To summarize research of empathy and cognition gains in the classroom.

1. Define teacher empathy for students.
2. Define student cognitive gain.
3. Describe procedure used for research.
4. Describe outcome of research.

Growing with the Team

Carl used this same type of systematic planning for each day's training. Thus, he planned each step and when variations were needed he was able to plan new ones as the training proceeded. Each step was planned so that it led to success for his trainees.

In another study, Carl served as the supervisor for a principal who wanted to use skills training in his school which involved all black children from the lowest socioeconomic group. The principal contacted Carl, who skillfully guided him through the program. The outcomes revealed that all the teachers improved in their use of empathic understanding as well as their application of systematic curriculum construction. That is, the teachers were delivering facts, concepts, principles, skills, and learning programs to their students. In addition to the effective teacher behavior it was found that the students had fewer discipline problems, fewer absences, and they earned the highest achievement scores ever attained by the students in the school.

Throughout all of the studies conducted by his former students, Carl was doing some of his own research. Carl was measuring the effectiveness of their work in terms of the movement toward the goal of enhancing human development. This was Carl's most important criterion, for to him if the technology led to a lessening of the human condition it was at best worthless. Carl kept his eye on the goal and kept reminding his former students of their progress toward it. Thus, he was applying his personalizing to his research. He was entering the Productivity Age by involving himself in policy decisions.

Carl's evaluation of his research was positive. He found the new human technology to be good because it enhanced the humanity of the principals, teachers and students in the schools that used it. Carl saw that thousands, perhaps millions, of people were using the human technology. It was exhilarating to see how human technology could extend a person's influence in a positive direction.

Carl knew it was possible for one teacher to be a part of a worldwide effort to improve the human condition. He also learned that technology is the preferred vehicle for extending one's influence. It was as if he could be fully interdependent with his fellow human beings. He did not need to be charismatic. Carl learned that effectiveness depended on systematic, substantive content which would be around a long time after he was gone. Thus, Carl also learned that his mission (to facilitate the growth of *all* people) could be maximized through systematic skills training.

Epilogue

Carl's personal effectiveness is rated highest in the emotional areas on Chart 5. Carl's level of physical functioning was limited by a medical condition. However, he maintained a physical program which permitted him to perform with intensity for short periods of time. Carl's emotional area was a source of strength that often compensated for physical limits. In the intellectual area, Carl focused upon concepts and principles and depended upon his students to develop ways to use them in their daily lives. Thus, Carl had to overcome an aversion to the systematic approach to learning and teaching when he entered the Information Age.

Carl was another learner who had a commitment to poetic approaches to learning. Originally, Carl had a very negative attitude about systematic learning. However, he was open to learning from his students and when they demonstrated the efficiency of systematic procedures, he expanded his thinking to include them. Thus, Carl was able to enter the Information Age as both a poet and a systematic thinker.

CHART 5
Effectiveness Chart for Carl Tatum

Dimensions of Personal Effectiveness

PHYSICAL	5–Stamina	④–Intensity	3–Adaptability	2–Nonadaptive	1–Sick
EMOTIONAL					
Motivation	⑤–Mission	4–Self-fulfilling	3–Achievement	2–Incentive	1–Nonincentive
Interpersonal	⑤–Initiating	4–Personalizing	3–Responding	2–Attending	1–Nonattending
INTELLECTUAL					
Learning	5–Acting	4–Understanding	3–Exploring	2–Involvement	1–Noninvolvement
Substance	5–Technologizing	④–Operationalizing	3–Principles	2–Concepts	1–Facts
Teaching	⑤–Individualizing	4–Goal-Setting	3–Diagnosing	2–Content	1–Unprepared

Dimensions of Teaching Effectiveness

Content Development	5–Skills Steps	④–Skills Objective	3–Principles	2–Concepts	1–Facts
Lesson Planning	⑤–Summarize Skill Steps	4–Exercise Skill Steps	3–Present Skill Steps	2–Overview Applications	1–Review Contingency Skills
Teaching Methods	⑤–Tell Show Do Repeat Apply	4–Tell Show Do Repeat	3–Tell Show Do	2–Tell Show	1–Tell
Teaching Delivery	5–Monitoring	④–Programming	3–Goal-Setting	2–Diagnosing	1–Preparing Content
Interpersonal Skills	⑤–Reinforcing	4–Individualizing	3–Personalizing	2–Responding	1–Attending

6 / Using Personal Power

Flora Roebuck

The Roebucks are a strong family. They are physically vigorous and intellectually bright, but most of all they are iron-willed. So, it was not unexpected that their first child was an unusually assertive young lady. Flora had a rare combination of physical, intellectual and emotional superiority which has been a mixed blessing because she threatens some people who are not as strong as she. Her voice is loud and firm. Her eyes flash. Flora is an imposing person.

Flora's home in North Carolina was congenial. Her mother taught school and her dad was a railroader who knew everybody in town. The family was comfortable in this small town. But Flora created waves as she progressed through school. For example, she was suspended from school for hitting a boy with a chair. She wrote poetry which was published in the small town paper and took first place in a Garden Club contest. Her essay against socialized medicine won first place in the county and third place in the state. When she attended the county medical association dinner to receive her prize, she embarrassed her mother by eating the

Using Personal Power

watercress and she felt badly for the second and third prize winners, who were also attending the dinner. Flora also won many academic honors. In fact, elementary and secondary school were really no intellectual challenge.

When Flora enrolled in the University of North Carolina at Chapel Hill she found her first real opportunity to expand her intellectual abilities. She enjoyed the whole experience, particularly marching in the band which played for football games and other campus activities. Even though Flora never understood football, she liked the music and the excitement.

Academic affairs went well at Chapel Hill and Flora graduated with honors in Creative Writing. She was the first female graduate to be so honored at the University of North Carolina. Flora wanted more intellectual challenges, so she enrolled at Cornell University for a Masters in Elementary Education, and she graduated with distinction. Her master's thesis was selected for listing in *Masters Theses in Education*.

Flora's career had been marked by a stream of skills acquisitions. She found she could quickly learn to do anything she chose to conquer. Her head was full of concepts which translated into action programs automatically. For her, learning was intentional, in that she sought it out. Her difficulty was that she always thought of more tasks where she could apply her skills. In many ways, Flora was a bundle of capabilities waiting to find a place to exercise.

A school superintendent in New Jersey spotted Flora during an employment interview and put her to work in an experimental, innovative program in elementary education. He knew Flora was "different" in the good sense of that term; he nourished her talents and skills. Flora recalled that she did not teach as her colleagues did, but somehow when tests were administered her students always made higher scores than the students of more conventional teachers. She tried to teach the essence of the material rather than getting caught up in irrelevant trivia. This was intuitive at first but identifying and teaching the essence of a subject soon became a skill.

Flora was retained by a national publishing company to prepare a skills-oriented, individualized reading program based on her master's thesis. For the first time she had to specify, for other's use, the reading skills she was teaching and the teaching methods she was using. It was a turning point in Flora's development because the concept of skills became firmly planted. From that time, Flora consciously delineated skills and designed learning programs for her students.

Flora Roebuck

Flora's academic brilliance was well established with everyone; but to her, the essence of teaching was the human relationship with her students. She felt their ups and downs and wanted to find some way to combine her humanity with the intellectual components of education. Thus, when she heard of the humane education emphasis at the College of Education of the University of Florida she enrolled for doctoral study at that institution.

The University of Florida lived up to its advance billing. It excited Flora with both its intellectual and its humane aspects of education. Flora studied with some of the nation's leading scholars in humanistic education, behavioristic education, and cognitive therapy. It was like being at the most plentiful and most delectable smorgasbord one could imagine. These were good years and Flora continued to acquire skills. The difference was that she was also developing new concepts and doing active thinking. In short, she was becoming a high-level contributor to the field of Education.

While at the University of Florida, Flora worked with a team that was training teachers to respond empathically to gain understanding. For the first time she saw a systematic way to improve teachers' use of facilitative behavior in their teaching. Flora helped to formulate the training modules and conduct the research. She saw it work and found it exhilirating. Here, she thought, was a practical way to combine intellectual skills with human skills. This concept formed in her mind and was to become a significant part of her life.

With some of her colleagues, Flora wrote a proposal to the National Institute of Mental Health for funding of a national effort to conduct interpersonal skills training in schools. This program was to have both research and training components, which meant that it would be on trial. Flora liked this aspect of the effort because it differentiated it from the majority of interpersonal programs which related anecdotes rather than research findings about their effectiveness. Thus, Flora's proposal focused on determining whether or not there was any relationship between interpersonal skills and academic learning.

The proposal was funded for $350,000.00 for three years so, for that period of time, Flora administered the National Consortium for Humanizing Education. She conducted teacher training. She managed the office. She kept track of the research. She also realized that every skill she had acquired in the past was of value in her direction of the Consortium. In fact, Flora was pushed to higher levels of skills in every area, especially

Using Personal Power

in mathematics. She knew a few elementary things about computers but the massive data base of the NCHE required sophisticated statistical procedures. So, as an intentional learner, Flora picked the brains of the local statisticians and computer specialists until she mastered complex procedures such as the modified Markov process.

Flora used her skills to teach skills to teachers. She developed skills programs for curriculum development, question asking, responding, empathizing, etc. Flora wanted to supply the skills training programs so very much needed by teachers. The number of teachers involved in the program multiplied by the thousands and soon an untold number of students were benefiting by her work. Whenever she had moments for reflection, it staggered her mind to think of the numbers of people who were being influenced by the technology she produced in her office at the NCHE. The most comforting thought was that the "hard-nosed" data revealed that human skills are related to intellectual skills.

For three years Flora had been in the "fast lane" of education. In addition to the work of the Consortium, Flora had made major addresses in 24 states, conducted workshops in 20 states, attended 50 conventions and written numerous articles for professional journals. It had been a bit wearying. Still, Flora could not help but smile when she reflected on the path she had traveled from North Carolina to the whirlwind days of the Consortium. It was as if her prayers had been answered beyond anything she had hoped.

At the conclusion of the three year study, the business of the Consortium had to be given an official accounting so Flora began a total audit of the program. The IBM cards which carried the raw data weighed one ton which meant that a lot of computer work had to be done. Slowly, the statistical analysis revealed that the teachers had made significant gains in their use of empathy in their classrooms. Also, these teachers had increased their levels of cognitive activities in the classroom. This included hundreds of teachers! That was a powerful finding.

The data for the students indicated that they had made (1) significant achievement gains (2) significant gains in the cognitive levels of their classroom activities (3) significant gains in their daily attendance (4) significant gains in their self-concept and (5) significant decreases in their discipline problems. The ripple effect had worked! A few trainers had affected the classroom practices of hundreds of classroom teachers and thousands of children had been helped to perform more effectively. Flora and her colleagues had made a real difference in the quality of education in American classrooms.

Flora Roebuck

Flora had been a major part of a thrust which proved that a humane technology could achieve humane ends. This was the first time in the history of humankind that this had been documented on a large scale basis. This was satisfying to Flora but she knew that other things lay ahead. She understood that the second generation of human technology was going to foster geometrically better outcomes from skills training. She had seen only the dawning of a new age in human development.

Flora's fame had spread across America and the rest of the world. She received invitations to consult with schools from every conceivable corner of the globe. As she answered these calls, she took the Human Technology with her.

As a next step Flora was asked to develop teaching modules for Texas' Right-to-Read program and she used her skills to combine human learning with intellectual learning. Hundreds of teachers across Texas used these modules to guide their reading programs.

Flora was invited to Johns Hopkins School of Medicine where she taught communication skills as well as medical information to unwed teenage mothers. The physicians were attempting to help alleviate this situation which affects the lives of 1.3 million teenage girls and 600,000 babies every year. They found that they could ameliorate the situation by using a technology which combined human skills with intellectual skills.

In a second task at Johns Hopkins, Flora conducted interpersonal skills training for physicians and nurses. Many of her students were from Third World nations and the results revealed that the Human Technology can be taught to people from other nations. These physicians and nurses improved their teaching skills significantly. Flora's sphere of influence grew and the systematic training with a Human Technology was her vehicle.

Flora found that she had to individualize her training program for the students who came from very different cultures. For example, one Indonesian student told her that she felt ashamed when she maintained eye contact with a man. At the same time, an Israeli lady was quite comfortable with eye contact. So, Flora planned two different programs for these students.

Flora created individual learning programs for hundreds of students as she taught various skills throughout the world. She was able to do this because she understood her substantive material, she understood human beings and she had the skill of developing individual learning programs.

Using Personal Power

Lesson for Israeli Female Student	*Lesson for Indonesian Female Student*
Course title: Interpersonal skills	*Course title*: Interpersonal skills
Unit: Responding to patient	*Unit*: Responding to patient
Topic: Positions of helper	*Topic*: Positioning of helper
Task: Eye-contact	*Task*: Eye-contact
Skill: Attending	*Skill*: Attending

1. Look at helpee's eyes.
2. Maintain position for 10 seconds.
3. Relax.
4. Look at helpee's eyes as long as is comfortable.
5. Relax.
6. Look at helpee's eyes and note the movements of their eyes.
7. Record the time you can maintain eye contact comfortably.
8. Repeat observation periods until you can maintain eye contact comfortably for 15 min.

1. Look at helpee's forehead.
2. Maintain positions for 10 seconds.
3. Relax.
4. Look at helpee's forehead as long as is comfortable.
5. Relax.
6. Look at helpee's forehead and note the movement of their eyes with your peripheral vision.
7. Record the time you can observe the helpee's eye movement with your peripheral vision.
8. Repeat observation period until you can observe helpee's eye movements comfortably for 15 min.

Having been successful throughout America, Flora began to expand into the rest of the world. She trained midwives and nurses in Indonesia. She took her work to Germany and Switzerland. She addressed scholarly groups in Israel. Amazingly, the human technology was being used in those distant places and some research in Germany confirmed the original findings of the Consortium. Thus, Flora was impacting a large segment of schools around the world.

Flora's success seemed like a fairy tale but there were moments of struggle and deep despair. The hardest times came when she knew what could be accomplished through the systematic application of a Human Technology and yet political forces prevented its use. In fact, political forces are the major subject of her study at this time. In previous work she had found that principals of elementary schools were the chief source of variability in the outcomes of programs in their school. Using this same model Flora is examining the effect of college administration upon the levels of effectiveness of their instructional programs.

Flora Roebuck

The Information Age is upon us and in her characteristic style Flora is entering it with enthusiasm. She has learned that human beings may be overwhelmed with the impending deluge of data unless they master the skill of processing the data. That is, they must learn to filter through the data and retain relevant information while discarding the irrelevant input. Thus, she is editing a book which deals with the problems of the Information Age. Simultaneously, she is embarked upon learning to use microcomputers. And, once in a while, she recreates herself with a pause for writing poetry.

Flora has used human technologies for interpersonal skills, intellectual skills, and physical skills. These have worked for her in a wide variety of settings. Now, another generation of the human technology has been created. It deals with human productivity and is geared to help people cope effectively with the Information Age. The fundamental skills are still effective because they are the basis for all human activity. However, the new human technology skills focus on productivity and are of necessity more complex. So, Flora presently is trying to teach these skills to some colleagues in education. The current problems seem larger than the preceding ones but Flora continues to learn. From her past record we can predict that she will find a way to get the new learning from her present situation.

Flora has invested her vast reservoir of human resources in education. She has completed research which will retain a significant place in the history of Education. She has left an impact on a large part of the human race. She is sustained by her mission which is to develop a skills approach to all educational situations. In short, Flora is a winner who belongs among the best and the brightest teachers.

Epilogue

Flora's personal effectiveness is assessed on Chart 6. Flora has had a continuing problem with weight and has attempted many programs to solve it. However, since she has huge resources in other areas, she is able to maintain a superior level of productivity. This raises two issues (a) what would be her level of productivity if she improved her physical functioning; and (b) how long can she maintain her current level of productivity? Only time will answer these questions, but for the present, her medical advisors are urging her to lose weight.

Using Personal Power

Flora has demonstrated her teaching skills in settings around the world. There can be no doubt that she is a master teacher. However, Flora's situation demonstrates a common problem for master teachers, namely that they have a need to express themselves in creative ways. Flora often finds herself caught in other people's needs for someone to do their routine work. Thus, Flora struggles almost constantly with the task of keeping herself free to do the high quality teaching of which she is capable.

CHART 6
Effectiveness Chart for Flora Roebuck

Dimensions of Personal Effectiveness

PHYSICAL	5–Stamina	4–Intensity	③–Adaptability	2–Nonadaptive	1–Sick
EMOTIONAL					
Motivation	⑤–Mission	4–Self-fulfilling	3–Achievement	2–Incentive	1–Nonincentive
Interpersonal	⑤–Initiating	4–Personalizing	3–Responding	2–Attending	1–Nonattending
INTELLECTUAL					
Learning	⑤–Acting	4–Understanding	3–Exploring	2–Involvement	1–Noninvolvement
Substance	⑤–Technologizing	4–Operationalizing	3–Principles	2–Concepts	1–Facts
Teaching	⑤–Individualizing	4–Goal-Setting	3–Diagnosing	2–Content	1–Unprepared

Dimensions of Teaching Effectiveness

Content Development	⑤–Skills Steps	4–Skills Objective	3–Principles	2–Concepts	1–Facts
Lesson Planning	⑤–Summarize Skill Steps	4–Exercise Skill Steps	3–Present Skill Steps	2–Overview Applications	1–Review Contingency Skills
Teaching Methods	⑤–Tell Show Do Repeat Apply	4–Tell Show Do Repeat	3–Tell Show Do	2–Tell Show	1–Tell
Teaching Delivery	⑤–Monitoring	4–Programming	3–Goal-Setting	2–Diagnosing	1–Preparing Content
Interpersonal Skills	⑤–Reinforcing	4–Individualizing	3–Personalizing	2–Responding	1–Attending

7 / Combining Strength and Facilitation

Andy Griffin

You have to be aggressive to survive in a family of sixteen children; particularly if you are a middle child in a family of sixteen. Andy is aggressive and/or assertive, whichever term you prefer. He is intellectually bright, physically strong and emotionally together.

Andy did not always possess superior physical abilities and he recalls many times when his older sisters punished him for his mischievous behavior. He laughs when he recounts the story about the time his dad decked him for giving his sisters a hard time when his parents were out for the evening. Andy's dad is a big man who rules his family with a firm hand. Since the Griffins lived in a fairly poor section of town, Andy's parents knew that he would have to be tough to survive, so they did not baby any of the kids. Andy knew this toughness was an act of love by parents who were preparing him for the cold realities of the days ahead.

Andy was gifted in athletics and his physical power was his forte. As would be expected Andy's high energy level made him a leader in all the neighborhood's various and nefarious activities. Thus, Andy learned to make it in the streets where he led most of the group activities.

Combining Strength and Facilitation

After graduating from high school Andy volunteered for the U.S. Marines because he wanted to be part of the best.

Camp was rough and Andy relates one story which illustrates his quick physical and intellectual power. It seems that a D-I called Andy to fight with a recruit much larger than he. When the bigger guy paused to remove his fatigue jacket before fighting, Andy seized the opportunity to jump on him while his arms were immobilized by the garment. He pressed his advantage and beat the other recruit badly. Now, this is not fighting according to Roberts' Rules of Order, but it is applying the law of the streets. The fight was not fair in the first place, so Andy adapted to the situation. This attitude has served him well in many conflicts.

College seemed a little unreal for Andy but since American International College was close to home, he gave it a try. AIC needed a good running back for its football team and Andy had grown while in the Marines. So, he enrolled at AIC as a 200-pound fullback who stood 6'1" tall. Andy majored in football where he achieved all-conference honors. College was a fun time for Andy who soon learned all the ways to beat the system. Since he had to declare a major, Andy enrolled in physical education where he qualified for a teaching certificate. Even though he worked hard in athletics he knew that he had not made a full effort in football, so he looked forward to professional football which would push him. When Andy graduated from AIC the Green Bay Packers were in their heyday and their coach was the renowned Vince Lombardi.

He knew of Lombardi's reputation for rock hard football and his "no nonsense" way of handling his players. It was clear to Andy that Lombardi was the only coach who would get the best out of him, so he went to Green Bay's training camp as a free agent.

Free agents have a rough time at any professional football camp, but especially so at Lombardi's Green Bay pre-season training. Andy recalled the good feeling of the football helmet which was made especially to fit his head. He smiled as he told of the time that the great Paul Hornung met the rookies at a local night spot and told the waiter to give free drinks to all the rookies. Andy said, "Hornung had real style." Perhaps Andy's most vivid memory was of a remark to him by Coach Lombardi. Andy was running the ball when he was tackled in the open field by one man and Lombardi yelled at him, "Big man, you should never be tackled by one man." This gave Andy a picture of how Coach Lombardi regarded him as a football player.

It's tough to make professional football teams, and most players who try fail to earn a place on the roster. Still, it hurts everyone who is cut from the team and this was especially true of Andy when they informed him he was to be released. The club officials told him of their disappointment at not being able to keep him and told him of an opening with another team where he was sure to make the squad. Andy said, "No, Coach Lombardi is the best in the business and if I cannot play for him I'll retire." So Andy returned to Springfield to start a new way of life.

Since he had a teaching certificate in physical education, Andy spoke to the officials at AIC and Springfield public schools to see if they had an opening. Sure enough, there was a position which called for both coaching and teaching responsibilities. Thus, Andy began his career as a professional educator.

As you might expect, Andy had many memorable experiences early in his teaching career, but one that stood-out was with his football team. Andy noticed that many of the kids who came out for the team were too small to compete effectively. Still, these boys had spirit and desire which the team needed and besides, they needed a chance to be a part of the team. So, Andy formed a special team of these smaller boys who entered the game as a unit for certain situations. Often they would enter the game at crucial moments and almost invariably they would make a spectacular play. Their morale was high and they soon gained status among their fellow students. Thus, Andy had transformed the "have nots" into "somebodies." Perhaps Andy's memories of the days when he was physically small helped him relate to these boys.

Andy's influence throughout his community led AIC to invite him to assume a leadership role in a center for the training of non-college as well as college people. This opportunity came at a time when the nation was in the midst of its civil struggle. Andy had marched with Martin Luther King Jr. when people had hurled physical and verbal abuse at him. He had felt his body surge when he held back from hitting people who taunted him. Now, he had a chance to use his training to help improve the community he had known for so long.

While working in the community center Andy met people who were to change his life. In a sense Andy was a diamond in the rough, but it took the best he had to reach into himself and say to others that he could learn from them. Specifically, he had to admit that he could learn more effective ways to help his own community. Sure, Andy knew every street and house, but he needed to learn subtle ways to break the cycle of poverty in the community. Andy was a prideful black man who had always met his people face-to-face. He stood tall and strong and clean. He had never bowed to any person. He knew he was equal to any white person. He also

Combining Strength and Facilitation

knew that his brothers and sisters were watching him to see if he would sell out to the "honkies."

Andy resolved his dilemma as only fully alive people can. He found a common ground with his white mentors and worked with them there. Andy knew the community so he taught his colleagues about the folkways. The mentors knew of ways to develop effective skills programs for the community so Andy learned them. Thus, strong, bright, and motivated people from the black and white community joined hands in a quest to develop skills to free others from the grasp of poverty.

The community center provided a million lessons for everyone involved in it. Perhaps the first was that if you are going to teach people you must relate to their world effectively. In short, you must show them that you can make it in their world better than they can, so they see your alternative lifestyle as a choice. This means if you are kind to other people it is your choice rather than a cowardly retreat from a fight.

One vehicle Andy and his colleagues used was basketball, one of the main games of the ghetto. They joined teams and consistently beat others who had more physical prowess. In this way they showed some of the best physical talents in America that you have to take care of your body in order to perform optimally. It was not uncommon to find several members of the teams intoxicated or "high" on drugs. Without making a major issue of physical health, Andy and his people demonstrated that a "high" player cannot get the job done when the going gets tough.

Andy soon learned that modeling was one of the greatest sources of learning. He found that his trainees watched his every move and they looked for inconsistencies in order to write him off. It was uncomfortable at first but he discovered that the Chinese proverb was right, "I hear and I forget, I see and I remember, and I do and I learn." So, Andy told his trainees about skills, lived the skills himself, and he helped them practice the skills. As a result of his work he saw miracles happen. Andy saw pimps, convicts, prostitutes, drug addicts and pushers become constructive people. The things he saw were difficult for him to believe, even though he worked hard to make them occur. He started to think that there might be hope for the human race, at least for people who would work and pay the price.

One of the best features of the training programs was that Andy's brothers were part of it. In fact, one of the most meaningful moments of training took place between Andy's black-activist brother and the white trainer. During one of the training sessions Andy's brother felt that the trainer was making too much headway with his black brothers so he stood

Andy Griffin

to his full height of 6'3", pointed his long finger at the trainer and at the top of his loud voice he said, "Hey man, do you dig black? I mean *black* black." The trainer looked at him and the room grew silent for several seconds. Slowly the trainer said, "I know only that there are two kinds of people, talkers and doers. I'm a doer." The room stood silent once more for several seconds. Andy watched, knowing it was a testing time for both his brother and the trainer. Finally, Andy's brother sat down slowly and the trainer continued with the training. Andy knew that everyone had won in that confrontation. Many years later his brother related that this was a positive turning point in his life.

Andy learned to make empathic responses, personalize problems, plan action programs, consult with community programs, identify concepts, identify problems, specify skills, devise skills programs, etc. For the first time in his life Andy was being pushed intellectually in ways that made sense to him. As he traveled across America telling others about the program at AIC, he got a strong feeling that he could meet anyone from any level of society and enter into a constructive relationship with them so that each of them could both teach and learn.

On the other hand, he also understood that he was a man, a full person who did not have to take less than he deserved from anyone. He had grown very large physically, emotionally and intellectually.

It would have been easy for Andy to stop growing, but growing had become his lifestyle. So, just as he understood his size he also knew that he needed credentials to support his growth potential. Thus, Andy enrolled at Harvard University to earn his doctorate in Education. Harvard was unthinkable in his early days, but now it was a natural step for Andy. He learned the ways of Harvard as well as the course content.

Still, Andy reached across cultures to join them. Unlike many people who have growth opportunities, Andy retained his old identity and grew to encompass Harvard as well. Thus, he graduated with his doctorate as a proud, strong black man, who wanted to use his skills to help people. It's only 90 miles from Springfield to Cambridge, but culturally it was many large steps. Several years later Andy laughed and said, "I'm the luckiest person in the world. I meet the right people at the right time."

Many Harvard men go to Washington to work in the government. In fact, the "Harvard Mafia" is an actual power base in D.C. But Andy used a different vehicle to go to Washington. He joined the National Educational Association as a training consultant. In this role he traveled across the United States helping teachers learn skills they could use in

Combining Strength and Facilitation

their teaching. Again, Andy learned more skills. He learned the LEAST model for discipline. He learned teaching delivery skills. He learned lesson planning skills. He learned curriculum development skills. He learned skills, skills and more skills! Andy learned skills, taught skills and preached skills. He advocated skills throughout America because he knew they delivered benefits to the people who needed them so critically. Also, Andy continued to model human skills because he knew that people must see skills before they can apply them. Andy had become a national leader. He continued to grow.

As Andy taught teachers about classroom management he conducted training in the LEAST model of discipline. The steps in this model are as follows:

L—leave the behavior alone
E—end the behavior
A—attend and respond to the behavior
S—state your goal
T—track the behavior (keep record)

During his classroom instruction of teachers, Andy planned his lessons so that he reviewed the prior lesson, overviewed the lesson for the day, presented the lesson in skill steps, gave opportunity for the teachers to exercise the skills and provided a summary experience. Andy had learned the ropes of teaching and now, he was giving them to his colleagues with the ROPES method.

Occasionally Andy would pause to assess his own effectiveness to see if his training programs worked for others. For example, he attended a 10th year reunion of a program for managerial people. It was amazing to see the people who were considered difficult cases just a few years ago. All of them had achieved more than anyone would have predicted. Some of them were business executives. Some were public servants. One of them was in the state legislature. The program had worked. There was no way to research the program precisely except to say that 100% of the trainees had succeeded everyone's expectations for them. The human quality of the program was beyond description. It made Andy smile inside as well as out. He felt joy beyond description.

Andy also recalled the National Consortium for Humanizing Education in Monroe, Louisiana, where he had trained black and white teachers, supervisors, and administrators. Andy remembered training these educators in Monroe, Baton Rouge, Waco, Fort Worth and Atlanta.

Andy Griffin

The voluminous data from this project revealed that the teachers had made gains in their teaching skills and more importantly, their students achieved significantly more than those of untrained students. These results had cleared the air as to the positive value of skills training for teaching.

Andy looked at the data from prisons where he had trained guards and prisoners and saw that both groups had made gains. He found that adolescents from the Rhode Island School for Boys had 75% less recidivism than boys from similar homes in other states. Studies from federal prisons revealed similar findings.

Teacher training groups from across America reported positive gains in skills acquisition. Andy was teaching skills which were increasing student performance in schools throughout the nation. He was conquering ineffective teaching with skills. He was helping the people who would pay the price of hard work.

Andy came to understand that he was an example of what could happen in America. He started in a low economic group and moved to some of the highest levels in America. He saw that his best football coaches had taught him the skills of the game. He reflected that his best teachers had focused on the skills of learning. It was clear to him that his best instruction happened when he was using his teaching skills to teach skills to his students. On the other hand, Andy knew that some of the people who had not gained skills were trapped in their limited worlds. It seemed to him that the basic race in the world was between skills and ignorance. If skills won the race there was hope for mankind.

Andy has seen the positive effects of a wide range of skills programs developed by Robert Carkhuff. He has seen them work for teachers, students, administrators and parents. He has seen their effectiveness in ghettos and middle class communities. He has seen them work with blacks, whites, browns, yellows and reds. He knows their power.

Andy also reflected on the message of Martin Luther King, Jr. and how he spoke of his dream. Andy saw the hopelessness of some of those who watched the civil rights marchers in Springfield. He felt the loss of a brother. He has known the fullest love of his comrades in battle. He has felt a tingle as he saw the national Capitol and the Washington Monument. Andy has known deep love as he helped his children make their life choice. He has known the pride of blackness. Also, he's known the joy of victory over poverty and ignorance. Through all of his pursuit of life Andy kept his faith in skills as the vehicle for human fulfillment. So, today

Combining Strength and Facilitation

he plunges forward with an enthusiasm for life. Each day he exercises, he studies, and he teaches skills. He hopes that others will hear his teaching and learn from him. Together they can build a better world.

Epilogue

Andy's personal effectiveness is extraordinarily high. His physical stamina enables him to apply his emotional and intellectual skills at a phenomenal rate. To most observers it seems that Andy always has "plenty of time." He makes things look easy. Andy has not abused his physical health; in fact, he has protected it zealously with a carefully developed physical program. Also, Andy has not allowed himself to be abused by anyone. He is willing to help others, but he is not a "bleeding heart" for humanity.

Andy's teaching skills have been demonstrated throughout America and he has stood the test of replicability. He can produce positive results wherever he goes. While he is a proud black man, he demonstrates over and over again that skills allow us to transcend race, sex and ideological differences. As Andy says, "I am fundamentally a learner. Everywhere I go, I enter the situation to learn." Certainly his outcomes indicate that he has learned a great deal.

Chart 7
Effectiveness Chart for Andy Griffin

Dimensions of Personal Effectiveness

PHYSICAL	⑤–Stamina	4–Intensity	3–Adaptability	2–Nonadaptive	1–Sick
EMOTIONAL					
Motivation	⑤–Mission	4–Self-fulfilling	3–Achievement	2–Incentive	1–Nonincentive
Interpersonal	⑤–Initiative	4–Personalizing	3–Responding	2–Attending	1–Nonattending
INTELLECTUAL					
Learning	⑤–Acting	4–Understanding	3–Exploring	2–Involvement	1–Noninvolvement
Substance	⑤–Technologizing	4–Operationalizing	3–Principles	2–Concepts	1–Facts
Teaching	⑤–Individualizing	4–Goal-Setting	3–Diagnosing	2–Content	1–Unprepared

Dimensions of Teaching Effectiveness

Content Development	⑤–Skills Steps	4–Skills Objective	3–Principles	2–Concepts	1–Facts
Lesson Planning	⑤–Summarize Skill Steps	4–Exercise Skill Steps	3–Present Skill Steps	2–Overview Applications	1–Review Contingency Skills
Teaching Methods	⑤–Tell Show Do Repeat Apply	4–Tell Show Do Repeat	3–Tell Show Do	2–Tell Show	1–Tell
Teaching Delivery	⑤–Monitoring	4–Programming	3–Goal-Setting	2–Diagnosing	1–Preparing Content
Interpersonal Skills	⑤–Reinforcing	4–Individualizing	3–Personalizing	2–Responding	1–Attending

8 / Giving It All

Mack Harris

The best teacher I ever saw was Mack Harris. He was the best by far. Yet, Mack was only beginning to tap his huge potential as a teacher. Mack Harris was six feet two and weighed 220 pounds. He had dark brown hair and a voice as deep as a fog horn. Mack lived with an intensity which defied description, and no one could be in his presence without realizing that he was exceptional.

Why was Mack Harris a great teacher? Because he had great teachers? No. Because he was a great scholar? No. Because he knew all the answers? No. Mack was a great teacher because he gave everything he had to teaching. He was honored to be asked to teach and he spent hours getting himself ready for each class he faced.

Mack never graduated from college. In fact, he had completed barely more than one year of college work. Mack was a master electrician who walked calmly into electrical crises that made strong men tremble. He strode among the oil wells of East Texas with a certainty that he could make their motors hum.

Mack taught electricians how to wire huge motors and he taught himself to cope with the newest improvements on them. He was confident

Giving It All

in his ability to teach others about electricity yet he felt deep humility when he entered classrooms and auditoriums to teach people about life. He was humble because he knew how important teaching is and he wanted to give students his very best.

Mack Harris taught about life and he used himself as an example. He told education majors about his "humpty-dumpty" progress during elementary school. He spoke fondly about the red-headed math teacher who made him work. It was with sadness that he recalled that teachers were thankful when he fell asleep in class.

Mack became emotional when he related that he had "totaled" 13 cars before he was 21 years old. He spoke with respect and regret about a judge who told him to either join the Armed Forces or go to prison.

Teachers sat spellbound as Mack recounted his days in the Navy when he held the cables that connected airplanes to the catapult on an aircraft carrier. He told how he had to roll from under the plane at the last instant before it lurched forward.

Teachers wept when Mack showed them his strong arms which had been broken while holding the catapult cables. His right arm had deep scars where it became infected with staphylococcus bacteria. Teachers could hardly believe that Mack had spent six months in isolation while they treated his staph infection. It was even more difficult for them to understand that the strong man they saw had become addicted to his painkillers or that he had been able to get all the booze he wanted while in isolation.

Mack explained his struggle with alcohol, and teachers found it difficult to believe that a person once buried so deep in debauchery could have turned out to be such a fine speaker. Mack wept when he told the teachers that he didn't want to hurt anyone else because he had seen all the pain he ever wanted to see.

Mack Harris tried to help teachers deal with an experience he had during a dream. He told them about seeing Jesus' face in his dream and that for the first time in his life, he had felt real love. Mack said humbly that this experience had turned his life around. From that time forward Mack tried to live constructively. The teachers often wept as they heard Mack's story.

Again, Mack helped them integrate the "mean" Mack Harris with the "re-born" Mack Harris. He reached to them in humility because he wanted them to help their students, especially the ones who were struggling with life as he had. Mack wanted the teachers to know that even the "worst" kids could be helped.

Mack Harris

When Mack finished teaching his classes, he was soaked with sweat. He had given all he had and he was very strong. Gradually Mack discovered that there were others who wanted to help people and he joined them. He joined the church, Alcoholics Anonymous, Gideons and numerous other groups. Mack wanted to be a part of every group that was "helping" people. He wanted to reach out his big arms and rescue everyone. Of course, some people were skeptical about Mack's turn-around but he continued to search.

Finally, Mack saw the work of Robert Carkhuff who had designed systematic programs for learning to help others. Mack read it voraciously and recommended it to others. It was like a new world. He began to talk about understanding how people show their love in a constructive way.

Mack wanted to enroll in school so he could learn more about human technology. The local university had to make a special ruling so he could register. The irony was that Mack had to be made a "special" case to enroll at the university where he had served as a guest lecturer and whose students called him their best teacher ever. All universities face similar admission problems but that's the kind of difficulty that arises from academic rigidity rather than pursuit of excellence.

Mack attended seminars where he heard national authorities speak about the possibilities of impacting the world constructively by using skills training. Mack saw no conflict between his Christianity and the helping skills. For Mack, the skills were a Christian technology. When the Bible said "In as much as ye have done it unto one of the least of these my brethren, ye have done it unto me," Mack believed that the helping technology showed him how to live effectively. The difference to Mack was that he offered his help in the name of Jesus.

Mack designed his own growth program which included: reading all the books about the helping technology, reading the "best" books about Christianity, enrolling in college classes and seminars which taught the human technology, working every day at his systematic physical training program and listening to Barry Bailey who taught the principles of a Christian technology on a Sunday morning television program. Mack agreed with Dr. Bailey and S.M. Fuster, S.J., who said that the Lord wants us to make use of all our human resources because they are His gifts to us, and we should do all we can to cooperate with Him.

Mack's initiative led him to think about ways the human technology could be taught to others. He knew it needed a sound financial base, so he planned to expand his company to several other sites in order to earn more money. Thus, Mack was growing personally and professionally.

Giving It All

His growth was not without cost and struggle but Mack was accustomed to that.

Mack intensified his teaching programs for those closest to him. He taught them about the importance of the Christian technology and of their place in it. He re-explored the lessons from his own life and tried to make it clear to everyone that as he had become a Christian and started to grow constructively he had turned his back on many of his old habits. He was sorry for having been involved in so much pain. He frequently said that even though he was not proud of his past he believed that God could use it. You see, Mack could talk to those whom people called the "darkest sinners" and respond to their humanity. For example, he once sat in a large distinguished church where poor and very rich both worshipped. One sector was reserved for the "street people." Mack looked alternately at the rich and the "street people" and then said about the latter, "I have a lot more in common with these folks than the upper class."

Mack was taken from us by an automobile accident. It was as if a football halfback had just broken through the line of scrimmage and gotten into open running territory. It seemed as if the best was ahead for Mack, but suddenly his life was over. Those of us who remain believe that he was taken on to graduate school where he can learn more of the mysteries he sought to understand.

Mack Harris still teaches. His life still sends messages to those who saw him teach. Mack was not perfect. He *was* deeply human. He struggled, he fought, he loved, he won and he lost, but most of all he lived.

Mack was unafraid for most of his life. His vast personal resources allowed him to move through life fearlessly. However, Mack finally came to understand how precious life is and then he began to experience some fear that it might be taken from him and those he loved. Mack had discovered a new world, but he entered it fully. As he once said, "I just committed it all to God. I used to say I would give it to God but, you know, he owns it all anyway." That's the way it was for Mack. He was a proud, strong man who could physically overpower any other man he met who wished to fight him. But, when Mack gave himself to someone or something he did so completely. He held nothing back. This scared others who gave less. So, it is easy for those of us who knew him to envision him, fully embracing life beyond this one. Someone asked him what he would do if he found that God was black. Mack did not hesitate. He said, "I will fall down and kiss his feet." This is how Mack taught—fully committed, fully open to his experiences as well as those of his students. When he taught he seemed as young as a little boy and as old as time itself. May it ever be so.

Mack Harris

The Beach And Sea
by
Mack Harris

I came to the ocean today.
How beautiful!
How much strength!
How much mystery!

The sand so white.
The water so blue.
I stand in a cove
And look at my feet.

I see only a small part of the sand;
A beach for my feet.
The waves come in
So strong and neat.

The waves so tall,
My feet so small.
But wait! My feet, my beach.
The waves have moved my beach.

What can I do?
My beach so neat,
It moves so quick
The ocean to meet.

I cry with pain
For my loss, you see.
It floats so far,
So quick it leaves.

I cry! I cry in fear.
My sand, my beach, my feet.
I move to find my sand you see
That has supported me.

But it's gone forever
To the ocean so deep.
But no, maybe
This is not the fate I see.

My sand may stay
Close for me.
I turn to search,
To seek and find.

Giving It All

My sand may stay
close for me.
I turn to search.
To seek and find.

My sand, my beach for my feet
To stand, to feel and see.
I look as I turn for there is
More beach and sand than I've ever seen.

Wait! Someone comes.
I call for help.
He comes to me
And help at last I see.

But what is this?
I hear his plea.
There is more beach
Than I can ever see.

We walk, we talk.
For all we seek is help
To be a keeper of
A mighty beach and sea.

So far we walk,
Our hearts are free
For the things
Our minds seek to be.

I love the beach
And the sea so free;
But now, more than beach,
My mind can see.

My friend, my sand,
My feet, Yes, all three.
We walk, we talk,
We plan to be.

I turned and found a man
So much wiser and so strong.
All the sand that was mine
Had left me so wrong.

We walk, we talk;
More help I find.
There is more beach and sea.
Much more than just mine.

Mack Harris

Don't leave, don't sway.
Let's find more help
More friends, more beach
So much more to find.

Thank you friend
For this pain and fear.
Thank you friend
For helping me find

The most beautiful beach
For all to stand,
to walk and talk and see
The mighty ocean strong and free.

Not some hungry thing
To rob from me
My sand so firm
But move with me.

Thank you God for the sand and sea.
Thank you God for a man
To be so strong and beautiful
Just as the sea can.

Thank you friend
For you and me.
The sand to move
Like you and me.

For man to help
To walk, and see
More sand to move,
More eyes to see.

I love the sand.
I love the sea.
But much more
I love the man I see.

With help and love
Our mission can be
To hear the cry
And make it we.

Our eyes must
Seek and find
Our mouths must share.
The help we find.

Giving It All

No one can be as great as He.
But help He sends for you and me.
Friends to share in love and pain.
No more a prison but a world of beach and sea.

9 / Putting It into Perspective

Summary

Education is in turmoil. While this is nothing new, the decibel level of the uproar is higher than usual. There are of course many reactions to the situation ranging from anger to jubilation. Perhaps most people are only hoping that all the noise will produce some constructive changes in education.

One reason for the increased decibel level is that the Information Age is making new demands on education. In the report of The National Commission on Excellence in Education, the members asserted that "learning is the indispensable investment required for success in the 'Information Age' we are entering" (p. 7). The report further stated that "the people of the U.S. need to know that individuals in our society who do not possess the levels of skills, literacy, and training essential to this new era will be effectively disenfranchised" (p. 7).

The report of the Carnegie Foundation Commission for the Advancement of Teaching entitled *High School* (Boyer, 1983) recommended that schools do a better job of what they have been doing. For example,

Putting It into Perspective

they advocated teaching for higher test scores, and better vocational training. To be sure, test scores decreased for a period of time, but there is still a vast pool of talented and educated people throughout America. In fact, the public's general level of education is much higher than ever before. In *A Nation at Risk* (Gardner, 1983) we read that "it is important, of course, to recognize that the average citizen today is better educated and more knowledgable than the average citizen of a generation ago—more literate, and exposed to more mathematics, literature, and science" (p. 11).

Most critics of education have missed the mark because they are using an outmoded knowledge of society as a reference point. They remember what school was like for them. They use that same mode of society as a standard for tomorrow. These perceptions lead primarily to erroneous conclusions.

Regrettably, the people who hope that education will be bettered by the recent efforts to improve it are going to be disappointed because the critics are addressing the wrong problems. For example, David Gardner, (1983) Chairman of the Commission on Excellence in Education, has been advocating changes such as more homework. The logic behind this recommendation seems very solid; however, when we examine it more closely we find it lacking. If schools adopt Gardner's recommendation they will probably teach students more of what they already are teaching and much of it is inappropriate for the Information Age.

The major impetus for many of the recent criticisms of American education stems from the fact that America has dropped from first place to last place in productivity among the industrialized nations of the world. Reflexively we looked to the first place nation, Japan, for direction in regaining our lead position. The report of The National Science Board Commission on Precollege Education in Mathematics, Science, and Technology entitled *Educating Americans for the 21st Century* (1983), stated "an obvious comparison to make is with Japan, because it is often viewed as a major international competitor and shares many of America's educational goals" (p. vii). In the same spirit the report of The Task Force on Education for Economic Growth, entitled *Action for Excellence* (1983), asserted that "Japan, West Germany, and other relatively new industrial powers have challenged America's position on the leading edge of change and technical invention. . . . The possibility that other nations may outstrip us in inventiveness and productivity is suddenly troubling Americans" (p. 13).

Thus, we began to consider seriously such things like placement tests at 3 years of age and pre-schooling for 2 year olds. Our collective

Summary

anxieties about not being good parents were complemented by our fears of not being number one industrially. Therefore, we panicked.

We took cues from other nations which maintain "tough" standards for their students. In many countries, a placement test is administered during the early teens and students are placed either in a vocational track or an academic track. Unfortunately, in America we have created one track for traditional students and another for "trouble making" students. The latter frequently is supported at a lower level than the former. John Goodlad (1984) concurred in this assessment. In his monumental book, *A Place Called School*, Goodlad assesses that "The decision to track is essentially one of giving up on the problem of human variability in learning. It is a retreat rather than a strategy" (p. 297).

Our nation was pushed further toward the Japanese model by our doubt about the efficacy of the democratic model in a competitive world. Individually and collectively, we had serious doubts that a democracy could compete with authoritarian states which make decisions quickly. As we saw the failure of many attempts to improve our society, it seemed that our way was hopelessly ponderous. We wondered if we had taken up the impossible task of educating everyone and we feared that the whole "boat" would sink unless we jettisoned the "burdensome" people, who some of us have accused of not wanting to contribute.

All of these factors threatened to make America shrink from its commitment to quality education for all of our citizens. We actually cut funds for educational necessities like school lunches. (You don't learn when you are hungry.)

But, all of the recent criticisms and "reflexive" changes contemplated or incorporated in our schools are targeted at reestablishing programs for the Industrial Age schools that don't meet the needs of today's economy. It is natural to shrink from a new effort when the recommendations for action are primarily re-cycles of things that did not work the first time. Earl Kelley often described our attempts at school improvement as working harder at what we already know does not succeed. Fortunately, today there are new things to try without totally abandoning the ideals of the past.

While we must look to the future for the resolution of our problems from the past, we must not forget our dreams. The dream of American Democracy is to help all people fulfull their noblest aspirations. In order to accomplish the highest levels of humanity, we must constantly develop higher order skills. This means that schools must teach higher order skills as humanity evolves to higher levels of fulfillment.

Putting It into Perspective

To move toward this aim, we must realize that the Industrial Age is over and that the Information Age is coming. Indeed, it is already here. For instance, over one-half of our economy is now derived from the gathering and dissemination of information. Naisbitt (1982) presented this fact cogently in his classic *Megatrends*. For example, he documented that in 1967, forty-six percent of the gross national product and 53% of income earned was accounted for by workers in the information economy, and the portion of the economy generated by information transfer/processing is escalating almost geometrically.

One Information Age requirement will be the need to increase the ability of individuals as well as machines to process information. Human processing of information means that people receive input and think about it before making a response. This means the S-R and R-S models of behavior must be replaced by S-O-R models. In the S-O-R model the O represents the process done inside the human being. Carkhuff (1983) explained that our responses should improve each time we respond. This can be represented by $S-O-R_1$; $S-O-R_2$; and $S-O-R_3$; etc. In this model, human beings must give up habitual ways of responding to situations and improve their responses iteratively by thinking.

Human processing calls into question most of the teaching methods used in today's schools. Studies reveal that 80% of the verbal activities in most schools may be classified as memory or the recall of facts. This means that by and large we are using S-R models of learning. This must change if our schools are to prepare students for the Information Age. Certainly, we will need some habitual ways of responding but the percentage of habitual responses needed for the Information Age will be significantly less than for the Industrial Age.

New data generation will be so rampant that one person will not be able to assess enough of it to be effective. Thinking teams will be required. The dawning of this reality can be seen in the Japanese style of management called Theory Z. They have learned that they need input from every worker in order to be effective. However, human processing is different from Theory Z input in that it requires more thinking. Human processing implies a higher and better response to each situation while Theory Z input may be a simple report of what is happening.

The Information Age is consistent with the evolution of humankind. It has been known for many years that humans have more brain cells than we use. Recent studies by Dr. Marian Diamond (in Aspy, Aspy & Roebuck, 1984) have revealed the amazing magnitude of the potential of the human brain. She reported that quite probably we have 100 billion

Summary

neurons and that each of them is capable of making 50,000 connections (Dendrites) with other neurons. The biochemical structure of brain cells indicates that each of them is more complex than our most sophisticated computers. Thus, we are just beginning to understand the structure of the brain as well as its physiology. The more we know about the human brain the more impressive it becomes.

Diamond's studies also revealed that the human brain must be nourished or it atrophies. On the other hand, if it is nourished, it grows. So, the great task for the human race is to use and nourish human brains. We do not know the limits of human brain functioning. We know only the principle that if it is stimulated it grows; seemingly that growth can proceed throughout a lifetime.

Schools that do not stimulate brains to higher-order cognitive processes (thinking, problem solving, etc.) are inconsistent with the Information Age as well as with human evolution. In fact, they are antithetical to both. The reality is that very few teachers stimulate the use of higher-order cognitive processes by their students. Mortimer Adler (1983) addressed this issue.

> Most teachers are currently trained to do only the didactic kind of teaching (telling). A relatively small number have been given some competence in coaching the intellectual skills . . . (p. 19).

Ernest Boyer (1983) writing in his superb book, *High School*, concluded that. . . .

> Most discussion in classrooms, when it occurs, calls for simple recall . . . . But serious intellectual discussion is rare (p. 297).

Since the Information Age requires effective teachers who facilitate human processing, we must be able to identify effective teachers. This process begins with the assessment of teachers in terms of their level of skills. That is, teaching is not only an art. It may not be a science at this time, but it is rapidly becoming one. Certainly, teaching is at least a scientific art. Thus, our task is to delineate those observable teacher skills which facilitate learning.

The first principle of effective teaching is that effective teachers are first of all effective people. Their personal effectiveness may be specified for the criteria in Table 1 (Carkhuff, 1981b). All teachers can be assessed for their levels of physical, emotional and intellectual functioning. Effective teachers will score at levels 4 and 5 for the human functioning scales,

TABLE 1
Areas and Levels of Functioning

Levels of Functioning	Dimensions of Human Potential						
	Physical	Emotional			Intellectual	
	(Fitness)	*(Motivation)*	*(Interpersonal)*	*(Substance)*	*(Learning)*	*(Teaching)*
5 ACTUALIZERS	Stamina	Mission	Initiating	Technologizing	Acting	Individualizing
4 CONTRIBUTORS	Intensity	Self-fulfill	Personalizing	Operationalizing	Understanding	Goal-Setting
3 PARTICIPANTS	Adaptability	Achievement	Responding	Principles	Exploring	Diagnosing
2 OBSERVERS	Nonadapt	Incentive	Attending	Concepts	Involvement	Content development
1 DETRACTORS	Sick	Nonincentive	Nonattentive	Facts	Noninvolvement	Unprepared

Summary

which means that effective teachers are first and foremost effective people.

A second principle of effective teaching is that effective teachers have a set of specialty skills which may be assessed by observing their teaching. These skills are marks of professional teachers. The scales in Table 2 were adopted from Carkhuff (1981a) for the assessment of teaching. Two aspects of the scales for teacher effectiveness require further explanation. First, some areas of the personal assessment scale overlap with the teacher effectiveness scale because the characteristics are found in both types of evaluations.

Secondly, the teacher effectiveness scales are cumulative so that in order to attain level 4 in one area, the teacher must have previously attained level 3, etc. This means there is no short cut such as doing the skill listed for level 5 while ignoring the skills at levels 1, 2, 3, and 4. A master teacher can exhibit the behaviors at all five levels, but the scores obtained from their teaching performance will be primarily at levels 4 and 5. In this sense, master teachers perform in the real world.

The foregoing standards for master teachers are high and it may seem that there are very few such teachers. But, there are some teachers who exhibit all of these characteristics, and their effectiveness can be documented. It is important to identify these exemplars in these days of extreme negativism since criticism leaves us with only negative direction. That is, at best, criticism tells us of things not to do. We need positive courses of action and people to demonstrate the skills to get us there. The previous chapters presented sketches of some educators who are exemplars of effective teaching. These educators are preparing their students for the Information Age by using skills which encourage human processing.

These sketches did not ask that the reader take leaps of faith. They documented the processes and the outcomes of actual classroom instruction by master teachers. Some of their work has been limited to small spheres of influence while others have had worldwide impact. Some of the skills vary according to the level of influence, but the core processes are the same throughout the world.

The anecdotal records of these master teachers are meant to illustrate the fact that they are thoroughly human. In everyday language, we might say they have a soul. They have risen above the tendency to be an either-or person. That is, many people encourage us to be either a phenomenologist or a scientist. However, these people are both phenomenologists and scientists. As such, they deliver their substantive content humanely. These educators are among the best and brightest America has to offer.

TABLE 2
Scales for Skills of Effective Teaching

Level	Content Development Skills		Lesson Planning Skills		Teaching Method Skills		Teaching Delivery Skills		Interpersonal Skills	
	Level	Skill	Level	Skill	Level	Skill	Level	Skill	Level	Skill
Master Teacher	5	Developing Skills Steps	5	Producing Effective Summary	5	Applying Methods (Transfer)	5	Monitoring for Effectiveness	5	Reinforcing the Learning
Effective Teacher	4	Developing Skills Objectives	4	Preparing an Effective Exercise	4	Practice Methods (Mastery)	4	Programming for Success	4	Individualizing the Learners' Goals
Minimally Effective Teacher	3	Developing Principles	3	Planning an Effective Presentation	3	Experiential Method (Doing)	3	Setting Learning Goals	3	Personalizing to the Learners
Ineffective Teacher	2	Developing Concepts	2	Formulating Effective Overview	2	Modeling Method (Showing)	2	Diagnosing the Learner	2	Responding to the Learners
Deteriorative Teacher	1	Developing Facts	1	Developing Effective Reviews	1	Didactic Method (Telling)	1	Preparing the Content	1	Attending to the Learners

10 / Exemplar Teaching

Some Afterthoughts

The preceding chapters have presented sketches of exemplary educators who are preparing their students for the Information Age. There are commonalities among these educators although each of them has some uniqueness. All of them use skills for their personal and professional growth. Their uniqueness is expressed in their special missions.

From *Clifton Sparks* we learned how a person can use their quest for human fulfillment to grow from a primary concern for one's own group to a generalized struggle for all of humankind.

John McFarland has shown us that neither war nor personal adversity needs to deter us from both our personal and our professional commitment to human fulfillment.

Marisa Valderas demonstrated that human concern can cross geographical boundaries as well as those of language and social class. She also depicted the triumph of personal spirit over adversity—not just to survive but to prevail.

Hila Pepmiller revealed that a person's religious belief can plunge her deeper into this world. She practiced the love of God by helping her fellow humans. Perhaps most of all Hila used the Biblical advice that "In

Exemplar Teaching

as much as ye have done it unto the least of these my brethren ye have done it unto me.''

Carl Tatum showed us how to grow with the times. He demonstrated that a person can flow with humanity by embracing new formulations as they make sense to his core values. Also Carl was concerned with the "passing of the torch" to the next generation. He realized that unless there is continuity with the next generation, then all efforts are in vain.

Flora Roebuck illustrated how people of immense personal power can commit their resources to a process that is bigger than they and by so doing can magnify their effectiveness geometrically. Perhaps Flora tells us most about the power of surrender. In a sense she found herself by losing herself. She empowered herself by assuming her responsibilities and allowing the seeds she had planted to grow wherever they will. Her crop has been huge.

Andy Griffin demonstrated that neither race nor sex nor social class need deter us from our quest to teach skills to other people. Andy also depicts the struggle of a super strong man to maintain his initiative while at the same time being responsive to others. He bridged the gap from a U.S. Marines Corps sergeant to a responsive teacher. Fortunately, Andy includes both of these aspects in his humanity. He can be both tough and tender.

Mack Harris showed us that great teachers are in process. They do not need to be "finished products," neither do they have to be elite thinkers. Mack demonstrated that great teaching requires a perspective that life is bigger than our classrooms, and that our students are as big as life.

The commonalities among these educators are their skills. All of them have used their training skillfully. Their personal skills areas are described in the following section.

I. *Physical skills—all of the exemplars have physical training programs* which was reflected in work which entails sustained high levels of effort. For example, Flora Roebuck who has a problem with her weight averaged sixteen hours of work per day for three years during the Consortium research work. Likewise the others ahd, and are having, similar periods of high level sustained work.

II. *Interpersonal skills—all of the exemplars can respond to their students and help them devise action programs to close the gap between their present worlds and the ones they desire.* In short, they can be fully responsive as well as fully initiative. Each of them has demonstrated their emotional skills during moments of deepest human experience.

Some Afterthoughts

III. *Intrapersonal motivation*—*all of the exemplars are motivated by something outside themselves.* They have missions. This means that many of their efforts are not understood by people whose motivation is for incentives or self fulfillment. These exemplars are able to choose tasks which continue their general direction toward their goal even though they do not advance their career in the conventional sense.

IV. *Mastery of substantive area*—The exemplars have mastered a substantive area and are continuing to do so as new information comes into their field. They are conversant with the facts, concepts and principles in the field and beyond those, they know the skills and the learning programs as well. This means that when they meet their students they know where they are cognitively within the substantive content in the field. This informed base frees them to meet their students easily and apply their human skills.

V. *Teaching skills*—*all of the exemplars can arrange their substantive content into its components and develop systems which deliver it to the students.* Also they have a variety of instructional modes so that they are not limited to one or two methods. Rather, each method can be utilized when appropriate and effective.

VI. *Learning skills*—*all of the exemplars know how they learn.* They are involved in meaningful learning. They begin by exploring the data and after a period of study they determine where they are in relation to their learning goal. Finally they arrange and execute steps to reach their learning goal. Their learning usually is considered to be easy by other people because they do it so efficiently.

The effective teacher also has specialty skills which can be observed.

I. *They can develop content* into facts, concepts, principles, skills objectives and skills steps. This allows for efficient delivery of the content.

II. *Effective teachers plan their lessons* so that they follow a skill sequence of review, overview, present, exercise, and summarize. The sequence gives each lesson a completeness so that the learner can form a gestalt.

III. The *teaching methods* used by effective teachers emphasize didactic, modeling, experiential, practice and application procedures. These move the learner from introductory to mastery phases of learning.

IV. The *teaching delivery skills* include diagnosis, goal setting, programming for success and monitoring for effectiveness. The master teacher assists the learner at whatever point he or she is in the learning process.

Exemplar Teaching

IV. The *interpersonal skills of effective* teachers include attending, responding, personalizing, individualizing and reinforcing the learning. With these skills, the teacher establishes a facilitative relationship with each learner. Thus, learning becomes a human process.

As they use their skills, these *exemplars became models for their students*, many of whom have gone on to pursue careers in education. However, the exemplars are more concerned about the mode of living rather than the goals. Like Dewey, *they consider human fulfillment a way to travel rather than a place to go.*

The exemplars do not depend on their scintillating personalities to dazzle their students into learning. They rely on solid substantive bases which they have developed into skills programs. Certainly, they use motivational techniques because they realize their importance in learning, but these are supplements to a solid base of skills delivery.

The exemplars let their outcomes speak for themselves. The data supports their effectiveness. They do not have to rationalize their lives. In a real sense they exemplify healthy behavior by "talking about what they are talking about."

The exemplars are in process. Each of them has changed many aspects of the way they teach. While retaining a core of uniqueness, their lives as well as their teaching have been shaped by the feedback they have received. In some instances they have made huge variations in their practices while in others they have made little or none at all. Their common lodestone has been a deep inner core of values which they have learned for themselves.

The common value of the exemplars is that people are ends rather than means. For example they see geometry as a means for more effective human living rather than an end in and of itself. Thus, they teach students about geometry rather than teaching geometry to students. They all agree with the elementary teacher who said that she taught students and would disagree with the high school teacher who said she teaches chemistry.

Each of the exemplars knows that life is a privilege to be valued above everything else in the world. They also know that it takes skills to live effectively. Thus, they implement their values through skills programs which they apply throughout their lives. This is not an easy path for any of them but it is their way to express their love for themselves as well as for humankind.

The beauty of these exemplars is that they live in the "real" world. In a day of disillusionment and cynicism, these people are not just surviving; they are prevailing. They are pathfinders who encourage others to join them in

Some Afterthoughts

the human march to fulfillment. They recommend that other educators examine themselves and make the tough but rewarding movement to a top quality delivery of skills to their students. If education will make that change, then the society will properly utilize its delivery to accomplish the dream with which we began. Fortunately, for a short while the choice is still ours.

References

Action for Excellence, 1983. Report of the Task Force on Education for the Economic Growth, Education Commission of the States.

Adler, M.S., 1913. *Paideia Problems and Possibilities.* New York: Macmillan.

Aspy, D.N., Aspy, C.B., & Roebuck, F.N., 1984. *The Third Century in American Education.* Amherst, Ma: HRD Press.

Boyer, E., 1983, *High School.* New York: Harper & Row.

Carkhuff, R.R., 1983. *Sources of Human Productivity*, Amherst, Ma: HRD Press.

Carkhuff, R.R., 1981b. *Toward Actualizing Human Potential.* Amherst, Ma: HRD Press.

Carkhuff, R.R., 1981a. *The Skilled Teacher.* Amherst, Ma: HRD Press.

Educating Americans for the 21st Century, 1983. Report of the National Science Board Commission on Precollege Education in Mathematics, Sciences, and Technology.

Gardner, D., April 1983. *A Nation At Risk.* Report of the National Commission on Excellence in Education.

Goodlad, J.I., 1984. *A Place Called School.* New York: McGraw-Hill.

Naisbitt, J., 1982. *Megatrends.* New York: Warner Books.